MANAGING
COMPUTER
PROJECTS

MANAGING COMPUTER PROJECTS

STAN PRICE

Price Project Services Ltd, Manchester

JOHN WILEY & SONS
Chichester · New York · Brisbane · Toronto · Singapore

Library of Congress Cataloging-in-Publication Data:

Price, Stan.
   Managing computer projects.

   Includes index.
   1. Electronic data processing—Management. I. Title.
QA76.9.M3P75   1986   004'.068   86–9212

ISBN 0 471 91113 5

British Library Cataloguing in Publication Data:

Price, Stan
   Managing computer projects.
   1. Electronic data processing—Management
   2. Industrial project management
   I. Title
   658.4'04   QA76.9.M3

ISBN 0 471 91113 5

Typeset by Photo·Graphics, Honiton, Devon
Printed and bound in Great Britain

Dedicated to my father—
Thomas William Price

CONTENTS

SECTION C   MANAGEMENT PROCEDURES

SECTION D   CHECKLISTS

SECTION E   CONTRACT CLAUSES

PREFACE

When I started assembling the ideas, concepts and data for this book, its publication was far from my mind. My original intention was to produce a personal *aide-mémoire* for my own consultancy and lecturing. However, I am grateful for Andy Hofton's suggestion that it ought to be published as an *aide-mémoire* for my colleagues in the computer industry also, and in a form where it would assist managers facing the problems of computer projects for the first time.

A deep debt of gratitude is also owed to all my colleagues and ex-colleagues in the UK and USA who contributed ideas, suggestions and corrections to the project. I pay particular tribute to my technical reviewers George Sudbury, Robert Burford and Denys Moody and my proof readers and literary advisers Sheila Moody and Rosemary.

My gratitude is also owed to the staff of John Wiley and Sons Ltd for all their help and assistance, also to the staff of Commercial Communications Ltd for handling all the correspondence connected with the book. Thanks are also due to Ann Trewin for typing the first draft and the Wordplex Bureau, Manchester, for word processing later drafts, and the staff of Manchester Central Library in assisting my researching. Finally, Brian Moore, Tony Dean, Margaret Jones and my brother John for their miscellaneous assistance and all those who had to put up with my constant thinking aloud.

Stan Price
Manchester 1986

CHAPTER 1

INTRODUCTION

The purpose of this book is to improve the management of computer projects. It is directed particularly at those managers concerned with the acquisition of software and hardware systems to perform functions for which they are responsible. However, anyone concerned with the supply and use of such systems should benefit from a better understanding of the various stages of provision, and the processes, decisions and constraints involved in each stage.

Much of what follows is common to all management of projects. Although computers have been in commercial usage for over 25 years, for a variety of special reasons the precepts and maxims of good project management have not been applied as well in this field as in many other branches of engineering.

It may be that engineers moving into computing have found the intangibility of software a difficulty while those who have spent their lives in computing are not trained in engineering project skills. Other factors that may have influenced the lack of good project management of computer systems are:

1. The digital computer by its decision-taking capability makes the specification of requirements a much more demanding excercise than in other disciplines.
2. Computer personnel are more prone than other professions to an interest in the techniques of their work to the detriment of the function their work is to perform.
3. Computers have a direct impact on the established working practices of people and organizations, which makes any mismatch between design and use very prominent before the project task is completed.
4. The very terms 'general purpose computer' and 'software' tend to imply a high degree of flexibility in the system which is the end-product. Flexibility would not be expected if we were designing a ship or a house, and similarly where medium to large software systems are concerned this flexibility is largely an illusion. Any looseness in specification which this flexibility illusion encourages must therefore be vigorously guarded against.

1

The specification and design of software systems therefore need to be at least as thorough and the manufacture at least as rigidly controlled as complex pieces of physical engineering if completion is to be on time and on budget.

Readers may gain the impression from some chapters of the book that the customer/supplier relationship is entirely an adversative one. This is not so insomuch as they have the overriding mutual goal of the implementation of a successful computer system on time and within (their own) budgets. The words in parentheses give the first indication of divergent interests towards that mutual goal. It is helpful for each party to know where these divergent interest could appear, and to that end they are clearly stated in the following pages. After reading this work, it will be realized that adherence to the principles and procedures laid down will minimize the chance that differences of interests will manifest themselves in conflict situations. If conflict does arise, the student of this book will know in advance what attitude is likely to be taken by the other party. The area most likely to fuel conflict is the interpretation of the specification and one must stress again the paramount importance of the system specification task.

The following chapters show the disciplines which must be enforced if project time-scales and budgets are to have a reasonable chance of being met. Like all good management textbooks significant attention is paid to the vital human factor. The book therefore defines as job titles the professional skills required at each stage to complete a computer project.

Finally it is important to stress that unless the stages laid down in this book are gone through it is highly probable that objectives and time-scales will not be met and budgets will overrun. Those involved in the estimating of computer project time-scales and requirements should elicit realistic esti-mates for each stage from those who have experience of what is involved and who will be personally responsible for each stage. Arbitary management decisions on both timescales and budgets are the quickest way of ensuring that not only will a project not meet its objectives but also that it will fall well short of them. Much of the advice offered may seem to be blindingly obvious. Remember that many projects and whole companies have failed because people ignored what, with hindsight, appeared to be blindingly obvious. Conversely, projects and organizations often succeed because the participants keep asking the obvious as well as the technical questions and not resting until they have a satisfactory answer.

Sections A and B of the book concern themselves with a description of the necessary actions, alternatives and constraints that apply at each stage of the project to the customer and the supplier. Section C describes the necessary management procedures. Section D gives checklists for items to be considered at each stage or in the documents appertaining to stages. Section E lists all the clauses normally introduced into computer contracts. Typical customer and supplier attitudes to each clause are described along with a suggestion for a mutually agreeable compromise where necessary.

CHAPTER 2

APPLICABILITY AND ASSUMPTIONS

The disciplines and the methods of ensuring these disciplines described in the following chapters are necessarily aimed at the larger computer projects. With medium and small-sized projects, while the disciplines must be adhered to, the methods may be less formalized, but if objectives are to be met it is better to be slightly overformal than to err on the side of informality.

There are many ways in which a project can be executed. This book is written on the basis of the following scenario. We assume that a *customer*, an organization whose main business is not computing, seeks to obtain a system, an assemblage of hardware and software, from a *supplier*. We also assume that the customer wants the supplier to have the responsibility for providing the system in a state where it is immediately ready to use. A contract of this type is known as a *turnkey contract*, a term which summarizes the idea that, as with a car, the customer should only have to 'turn the key' and the system is ready to 'drive away'. It will become clear, in the course of the book, that if the key-turning day is to arrive in a useful timescale the customer is going to have to do a great deal more than just choose a supplier and wave a cheque exchangeable for the 'key'.

Three other scenarios are considered and dealt with as digressions from the main theme, namely the customer uses the hardware which he already possesses or purchases separately and:

1. Enters into a separate software development contract.
2. Purchases a package (existing piece of software).
3. Develops the software himself, usually in his own internal computer department.

The book assumes that only manufacturers' production line computers, computer peripherals and communications equipment will be used. Except in extreme circumstances only manufacturers' standard products should be used for such software items as operating systems, compilers, file handlers, etc. The design process referred to means the design of systems by the selection and integration of standard items of equipment and software with 'special-to-project' designed software to perform a definitive function. The

3

4

design of computer and computer peripheral hardware, communications equipment and standard software such as operating systems is not covered.

The book also assumes that an organization independent of any particular computer project, will have a coherent computer policy. An extreme example would be an anti-technology job protectionist pressure group having a policy that no computer usage was to be considered. At a lower level an organization that has a large electronic maintenance organization and possesses a large number of computers of the same type may have a general rule that all computer hardware maintenance on that type of computer be performed by its own maintenance organization. General guidelines about a recommended software language for applications of a particular type may also be present in order to reduce expenditure on staffing and training. What I am saying is that there should be corporate guidelines which will simplify the research, justification, planning and implementation of new computer systems. Like all guidelines they should be capable of justified revision perhaps based on a fixed periodic review basis.

CHAPTER 3

PROJECT STAGES

The first stages of the total project are the concern of the customer alone. The first section (A) of this book is therefore directed to his organization and actions he must perform, namely:

Chapters A1–A3: the customer environment required for a successful project.
Chapter A4: the feasibility study.
Chapter A5: the customer's requirement specification.
Chapters A6–A8: choice of a supplier leading to contract signature.
Chapter A9: the customer/supplier's functional definition.
Chapter A10: customer's monitoring of supplier's progress.
Chapters A11–A12: customer's acceptance of the system and putting into operation.
Chapter A13: running of system.
Chapter A14: decision when to retire the system.

The supplier's view is in some ways a mirror image but he has different objectives, constraints and problems. Methods of defining these are described in the second section (B):

Chapter B1–B2: the supplier environment required for a successful project.
Chapter B3–B5: supplier's activities up to contract.
Chapter B6: the customer/supplier functional specification.
Chapters B7–B11: supplier's activities prior to acceptance.
Chapter B12: supplier's acceptance activities.
Chapters B13–B15: supplier's support activities.
Chapter B16: supplier's activities after acceptance.

Even with the scenario defined in Chapter 2 on which the project stages are based,the reading of the whole of this book will help each party to consider and understand the activities, and problems, of the other. This is particularly important if one of the alternative scenarios is followed. It should be noted that when the software development is performed in-house fresh dangers are introduced by the blurring of responsibilities, thus adding to the difficulties of project management. It will not always be the case that a project stage has to be completed before work on the next stage commences.

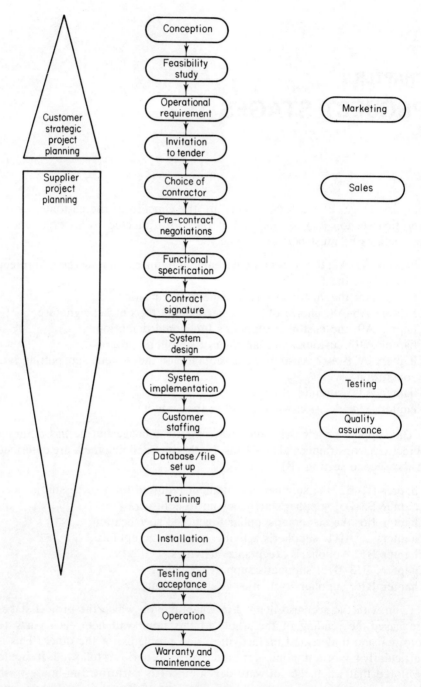

Figure 3.1 Computer Project Stages from Conception to Operation.

However, the strict sequence of stages should never be lost sight of. The sequential stages in the setting up of a computer system are shown in Figure 3.1. Figure 3.2(a)–(e) expands this into more detail, showing the connection between the various activities and the distribution of the responsibilities for these activities between customer and supplier. This shows the main scenario on which the book is based.

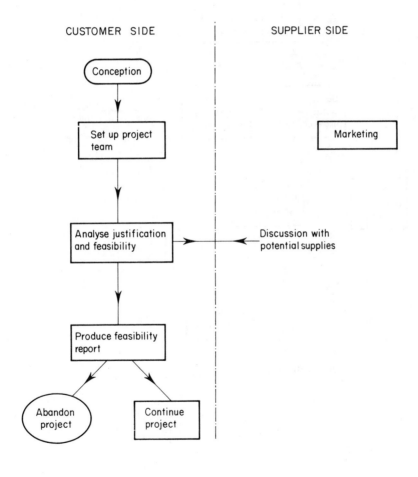

Figure 3.2a   Feasibility Phase—Stages and Activities.

8

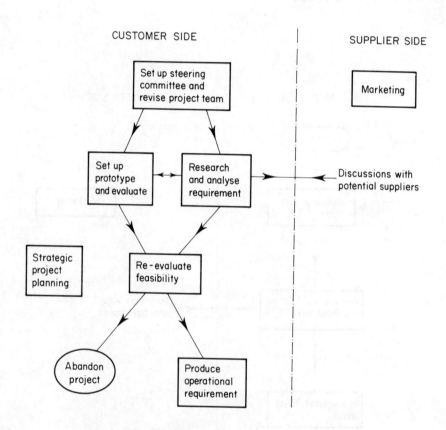

Figure 3.2b Requirements Phase—Stages and Activities.

9

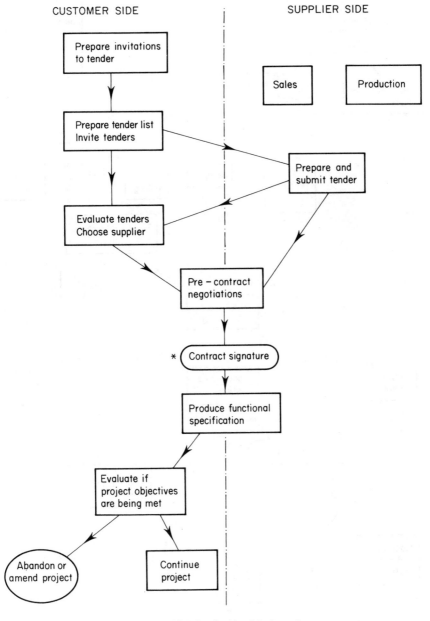

CUSTOMER SIDE

SUPPLIER SIDE

Prepare invitations to tender

Sales

Production

Prepare tender list
Invite tenders

Prepare and submit tender

Evaluate tenders
Choose supplier

Pre – contract negotiations

* Contract signature

Produce functional specification

Evaluate if project objectives are being met

Abandon or amend project

Continue project

* Possible for function specification / top level design only

Figure 3.2c Contractual Phase—Stages and Activities.

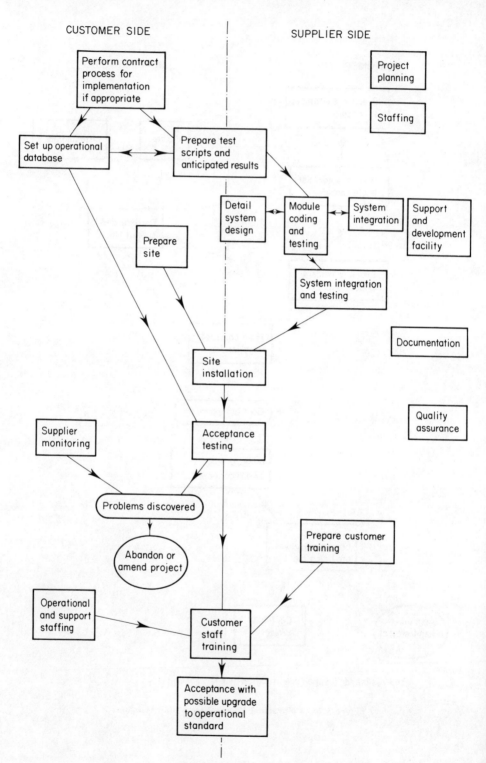

Figure 3.2d Implementation Phase—Stages and Activities.

11

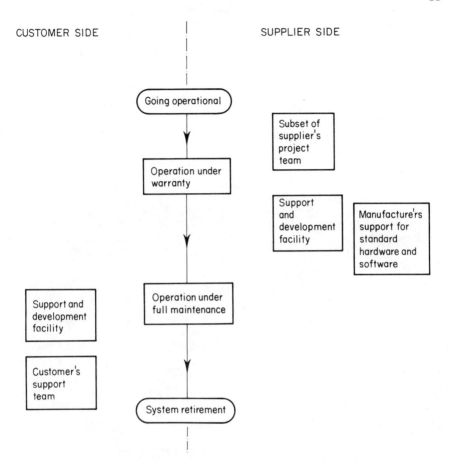

Figure 3.2c   Operational Phase—Stages and Activities.

SECTION A
CUSTOMER ACTIVITIES

CHAPTER A1

ORGANIZATION TO MEET THE REQUIREMENT

There are two principal organizational methods of meeting a user requirement:

1. Do it within the organization.
2. Get a supplier to do it.

Doing it within the organization assumes the existence of a computer (data processing or systems including engineering) department within the organization. Even though the very large projects could justify the setting up of a department to implement them, the added risks and increased timescales that this would mean are never justifiable.

Superficially the attractions of keeping it in-house are numerous; cheaper, more control, etc. However, the following should be noted:

1. The absence of formality and discipline that a contractual situation brings about quite often leads to looser specification and control.
2. An existing computer department will inevitably be biased to meeting the requirement by putting it on its existing computers, extensions to them, or computers of that type, without determining what is best or even suitable for the application.
3. The majority of computer departments have a bias towards commercial applications and are unsuitable for implementing non-commercial applications unless the analysis is a genuine combined user/computer department task.
4. Airlines, banks, defence establishments, etc. tend to have computer departments with the necessary systems and communications expertise for today's systems implementations. However, many others do not, and the typical computer department composed primarily of systems and programming expertise is not adequate.
5. The staffing of projects can also be a problem. The time taken to assemble a team is significant and may not be acceptable to the project timescales. Also, after the project is completed, unless there is another project to employ them on, one is faced with the question of how

they can be effectively utilized. (N.B. The use of short-term contract personnel gets over this problem and does not necessarily mean a lack of professionalism—quite often the reverse.)

Assuming the project is a large one with a high engineering and/or communications content, the following must be present before an in-house implementation is considered:

1. A large multi-disciplined systems department, including engineering and communications expertise, must already be in existence.
2. This department must have significant applications knowledge or the user department significant computer knowledge.
3. The systems department must have proven project control techniques and tools and preferably a support and development facility with adequate spare time and capacity (see Chapter B15).
4. The systems department and the user department must have sufficiently adequate spare manpower of all required disciplines.

Unfortunately, only the largest organizations can afford such a systems department. Even they will not always be able to set one up because of the job classification and demarcation issues that will arise where a multi-discipline department is set up inside a structured organization.

Therefore one is faced with the inevitability of going to contract. Even then multi-discipline teams are required to prepare the operational requirement; prepare the tender; evaluate tender responses; choose the supplier, etc. However, the problems of forming small teams for definite periods are somewhat less than those of setting up a department for an indefinite length of time.

Where teams cannot be justified and yet the project is of sufficient size for it to go to contract one- or two-man teams must perform the functions. They should have access to all the relevant knowledge. If some of the required knowledge does not lie within the organization, outside resources should be enlisted including consultants, but they should always be recruited with caution following the procurement rules laid down in Chapters A6 and A7.

It is sensible to ensure that there is continuity between the teams set up for each stage of the project. The mix of job skills required at each stage of the project is described in the chapter appertaining to the stage.

Whatever the composition of the team it should report, as with the requirement definition team, to a manager or management committee with sufficient executive responsibility positively to commit all the necessary resources required for the implementation of the system and its subsequent operation.

The steering committee should be responsible for setting, after advice, the functional, timescale, and financial objectives of the project. It should be responsible for revising these, if for instance, they prove to be mutually exclusive. The steering committee should be composed of all with a vested interest in the project representing operational, technical and financial aspects, although like all committees it should be restricted to ten members.

CHAPTER A2

FINANCIAL/COMMERCIAL CONSIDERATIONS

The arrangements that customers and suppliers agree for the payment of turnkey systems vary between the extremes of 'cost plus' and fixed price. 'Cost plus' is where the customer pays all the supplier's costs in supplying him with a system plus a fixed percentage for his profit. Generally this method of payment has fallen into disfavour with customers reluctant to give such an open-ended commitment. Often, however, the supplier is in great difficulty in quoting a fixed price because he cannot estimate the work content (principally special-to-project software) until after the design stage is complete.

A frequently agreed compromise is for the supplier to quote a fixed price up to the completion of the design stage with an estimation (often called a budgetary quotation) for the rest of the work. This is accompanied by an agreement that a price is fixed for the remaining work, at the end of the design stage. Customers may further ask that the initial budgetary quotation is accompanied with a limit of liability over which the fixed quotation for the rest of the work cannot rise. The same conditions could apply if the point at which the implementation price had to be fixed was the end of the joint functional specification stage.

Because of the timescales and values of large turnkey contracts, particularly where there is a special-to-project element, suppliers expect to be paid in stages. This is the normal situation that customers agree to, subject to the stage payments being set against identifiable achievements in the life of the project. Generally stage payments are shown as percentages of the overall contracted price. The agreement on a stage payment plan is governed by the supplier's desire to minimize the interest charges he incurs in the time between him incurring costs (particularly on high-priced bought-in items) and these costs being covered by payments from the customer. Against this the customer wishes to retain as big an inducement as possible for the supplier to perform satisfactorily especially in meeting timescales and, of course, he will be normally getting interest on the money he has set aside for the project which he loses when he pays the supplier.

The determining of a mutually satisfactory stage payment plan can only be done by a detailed calculation of both customer's and supplier's cash flows on the project. This will require a frank exchange of data between the two. The customer should differentiate when calculating the supplier's cash flow between the supplier's costs and the supplier's prices (costs + profit). It is also important to split equipment (hardware) and labour (mainly special-to-software) costs which will vary by different amounts over the life of the project. However, whatever the cash flow calculation shows, the customer should be aware that any interest charges he forces the supplier to incur will naturally add to the price quoted to him. It is normal for the stage payment plan to have the last payment (which can be up to 15 per cent) to be scheduled for when the system has been handed over and has operated satisfactorily for a period (up to one year).

Any changes to the specification will require their own payment terms and these should be calculated and agreed as for the main stage payments plan. It is sometimes convenient to time these to coincide with the main plan subject to this not significantly altering the financial picture.

All the above calculations should take into account the effect of inflation. How inflation is to be handled should be clearly stated in the contract. The contract can be truly fixed priced (firm fixed) in which case the supplier will bear the cost of inflation. In this case his contractually agreed price will *not* be varied to take account of inflation. The contract can, however, be 'simply' fixed price in which case the price will vary with inflation in a way the parties will agree contractually. The normal method is for the price to vary in accordance with the appropriate national indices for equipment and labour. If this is the method adopted all prices must be broken down into their equipment and labour components and the category into which each deliverable item falls shown.

Other measures can be considered by the customer with a view to making the financial cost to him more acceptable. However, many of these may be upsetting or unacceptable to the supplier, or he may adjust his price to offset them. The customer should also be careful that if he takes advantage of them he may give the supplier excuse for non-performance. The measures include:

1. *Bulk buying and Original Equipment Manufacturer (OEM) discounts.* It may be financially advantageous to buy some equipment items direct from the manufacturer without altering the vital total responsibility feature of the turnkey.
2. *Leasing.* It may be possible to lease equipment in part or in total, either from the manufacturer or one of the specialist computer leasing companies. The latter case may have the advantage of securing earlier delivery than from the manufacturer, as the leasing companies hold stocks and reserve positions on the manufacturer's production lines. Some leasing plans include a purchase option.
3. *Second-Hand Equipment.* It may be possible to purchase or lease second-hand equipment as a full or interim solution. Consideration must, however, be given to the higher maintenance requirements;

lower availability; lack of spares which use of second hand equipment probably entails.

4. *Hardware and/or software packages.* Manufacturers often offer such packages at a special advantageous price. Furthermore the purchase of such packages can result in having items which are superfluous to the project. These can be sold off with the resultant financial benefit to the project. (N.B. The use of the word package in this context means a set of hardware and/or software items. It should not be confused with the more general use of the word package, in the computer industry, meaning a standard item of applications software.)

5. Many customers will be paying for the project from budgets which are assessed annually. Sometimes it may be convenient for a customer to advance or hold back a stage budget for an internal budgetary reason. The usual one is to advance a payment before the end of the financial year when the budget out of which it is to be paid would be lost or require rejustification if it has not been used. This technique should not be entered into lightly without considering the aspect of a stage payment that motivates the supplier through his financial loss if it is delayed.

All these suggestions are not only for consideration at contract award time but should be regularly reviewed throughout the life of the project. The supplier will be doing this for his own commercial interest and there is every reason for the customer doing likewise.

Although this book concentrates on management procedures there is a place for straight talking between the customer and the supplier (including horse trading) at the right level on or off the record. However, this method of working will be complementary to the management procedures described and where possible agreements made in this way should be translated into action via the management procedures. At no time should off-the-record agreements conflict with what is documented and certainly it is an axiom of good management that except in extreme circumstances, at no time will senior management on both sides undermine their subordinates' authority for dealing with the other side.

Examples of the horse trading that could occur are the supplier giving way on some matter in return for the customer being a reference sale for the supplier at a future date. In this case what the customer is getting should still be introduced via a change request (see Chapter C1) which the supplier will then implement at zero or nominal cost.

Another example could be where a relaxation in response time specifications is offset by an increase in functional capability. Here the change request of the former will show an effective credit which equals the amount at which the change note for the latter will be costed. In a perfect world of course, in spite of the charade, both sides will still have done their independent costings.

CHAPTER A3

STAFFING AND RECRUITMENT

The importance of the customer's project team concept in the implementation of computer systems cannot be overemphasized. Internal politics which might destroy the integrity of the team are a significant factor in the failure of computer projects. Typical of these are a battle between user and computer departments for control of the project or, in some organizations, between a commercially biased computer services department and an engineering department rapidly expanding into digital techniques via microprocessors and communications.

As recommended earlier, the independent-of-department project team reporting to a steering committee is the best way of avoiding these problems. A possible structure is shown in Figure A3.1. The choice of the project manager is critical if an integrated team is to be welded together and he/she should be chosen for his/her ability to do this and manage administratively and technically rather than his/her membership of a particular department or discipline. A professional computer project manager has obvious advantages in doing this, although these can be offset by the objectivity of a user who will tend to be more correctly oriented to providing an operational system rather than satisfying some particular computer ego trip. The team that he manages should ideally be long on quality and short on numbers commensurate with an adequate number to do the job.

The team members can come from existing staff, staff taken on contract or newly recruited staff. Care should be taken in the existing staff chosen for the team to ensure that line managers have not taken the opportunity of getting rid of dead wood. All existing staff should have their former duties taken away from them sufficiently to ensure adequate attention is paid to their project duties. Most projects will see them completely dedicated to the project. The separation of the team from line disciplines can present problems to members of the team (particularly users) in terms of their career progression. Positive measures should be taken before the project team is set up to ensure that service to the project team is considered in the promotion equation. However, care should be taken to see that this is not overdone to the extent that vital relationships with other departments are impaired. The absence problem could be cured by having users serve only

21

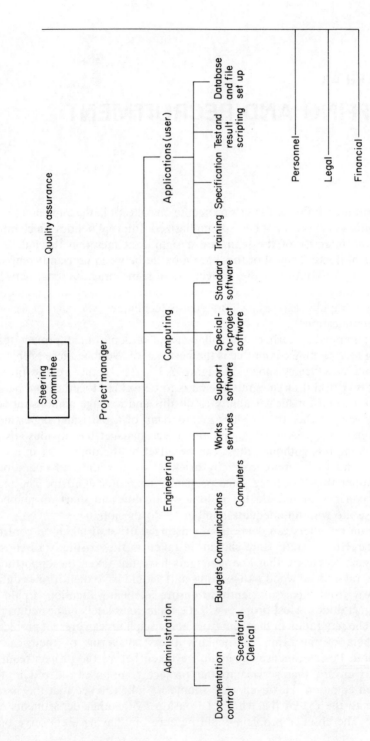

Figure A3.1 Customers Project Team—Possible Structure.

short terms of two or three years. This could also apply to other disciplines thus overcoming the staleness problems. Any policy such as this must allow some degree of staging and overlap in order to ensure continuity of the project team. Promotion could lead to key personnel being removed from the team, or if they remain in the team doing the same work as before. These might cause anomalies that a hierarchical organization would find hard to assimilate. These problems must be anticipated and a solution found which does not adversely affect a man's career or his pay. Recommendations for promotion should be geared to specific measurable attainments with the team and the organization's policy must recognize that work on the team is of at least equal value to work in the departments. The project manager, however, should serve through from conception to acceptance unless things go badly awry. A replacement manager always has the opportunity to explain away problems as being caused by his predecessor and as such is less motivated towards solving them.

Consideration should be given to the use of contract staff in the manning of posts within project teams. This is particularly relevant where the need is only for the duration or part of the duration of the project, or where the salary level that would have to be paid to recruit an individual with the necessary experience and skill would significantly distort the salary levels of a company leading to unrest among the regular staff. Contract staff have the reputation of being unreliable and indeed they have no need to be loyal to the customer nor to the project, and can always walk away. However, this reputation is not necessarily deserved and a contractor can display an objectivity which a recruitee, mindful of personnel considerations (not least his own promotion chances) may have to temper. A contractor also has his reputation in this particular field to consider. Where a contractor is employed to cover a function that will be required for a long period, the contractor's terms of reference should include the duties of training a permanent staff member, who will understudy him.

Where direct recruitment is undertaken for the manning of the project teams, this will normally be for computer and engineering personnel. Generally the user positions on the teams require applications and organization knowledge which is not available on the open market. Junior positions in the computer, and to a lesser extent, the engineering profession are particularized by a specific manufacturer's offering, software language, etc. Therefore the recruitment to fill the more junior posts generally cannot take place until a supplier is chosen. The more senior computer and engineering posts must be filled some time before a supplier is chosen. This permits them to add their knowledge to the choosing of the supplier and makes them feel committed to it, once it is taken. The recruitment of computer and engineering personnel will therefore have at least two distinct phases:

1. Recruitment of senior (management) computer and engineering personnel so that they are in post at least six months before the supplier is chosen.

2. Recruitment of junior (specialist) computer personnel phased after the supplier has been chosen.

For both phases, but particularly the first, the lead time before a person is in post should be pessimistically estimated. It should be noted that for organizations wishing to recruit computer personnel, it is a seller's (the personnel) market, and the computer industry generally exhibits different techniques and work patterns. It is probably prudent therefore that the recruitment programme is handled by an experienced computer recruitment agency or in particular cases a head hunter (this is an agency which given a particular job specification will use its knowledge of the market-place to approach suitable persons direct as opposed to advertising and hoping there are responses). The customer should still conduct his own interviews using the personnel department and project team managers.

The author believes that all teams should have clear written objectives. Unless there is clear evidence that the team is not working together, individual job definitions should be avoided apart from the team leader. He will have as his objectives the team objectives. It may also be necessary for contractual reasons to give clear job definitions to contract personnel.

The project manager will have as his job definition, the production of a system to meet the functional, timescale and financial objectives as defined by the steering committee. Any insuperable problems to him doing that, should, immediately they are identified, be reported to the steering committee.

Finally it must be emphasized that the personnel we are talking about will be responsible for choosing the supplier, monitoring him and accepting his finished product. It is appropriate that they do this because they will then go on to form the nucleus of the team supporting the operational system. As such they may have different attitudes from the supplier's personnel who may be development orientated.

The attitude of the relevant trade unions should be given consideration in all questions of personnel. They may be against the use of contract personnel for instance. It must be stressed, however, that project positions are normally highly specialized and cannot be filled simply on a head count basis. Generally the novelty of work on a *well-run* project does lead to a high degree of self-motivation, and problems with team members themselves are rare. This does not apply to the eventual system user, and it is advisable to take early measures to ensure that the unions co-operate in the operational use of the system.

A structure is suggested in Figure A3-2 for the organization responsible for supporting and running the system on a day-to-day basis after acceptance.

The Appendix to this Chapter classifies the disciplines that are relevant to computer projects. These classifications are of necessity broad and are to a limited extent subdivided. The intention is to give a feel for the job titles, skills and attitudes that must be brought together, at each stage, if a computer project is to be successful.

Training will be required for those users, computer, engineering, etc., personnel responsible for the support and day-to-day operation of the system

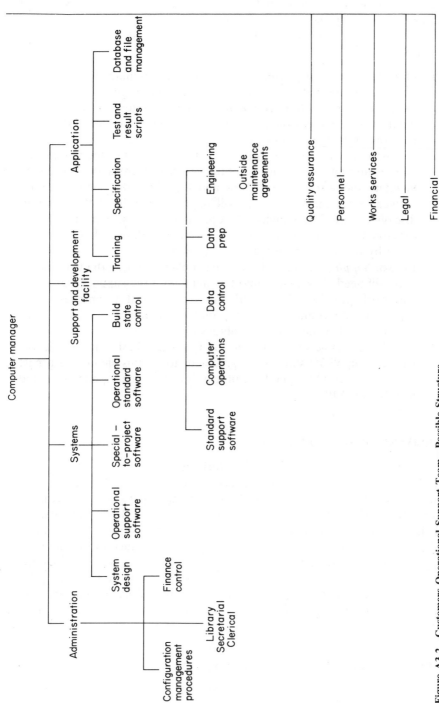

Figure A3.2 Customers Operational Support Team—Possible Structure

after acceptance. This will normally be provided by the supplier as part of the turnkey contract and therefore is described in Chapter B11.

Training will also be required for the project teams. This will fall into several categories:

1. *Management training*. General management training will be given, where it is required. A specific course should be given on the management of computer/communication systems and computer/engineering personnel. Emphasis should be placed on the work patterns of computer personnel.

2. *Cross-fertilisation between disciplines*. The members of the multi-discipline teams will need to learn a little of each other's skills in order to facilitate the work of the teams and especially the communication between team members. This will happen naturally if the different disciplines are intermingled in open-plan offices, but it may be expedited by short courses on each of the disciplines. These could be given by the appropriate team members themselves.

3. *Chosen Supplier Training*. Once the supplier is chosen the team members will need to become rapidly familiar with the supplier's products and work practices, particularly his management techniques. Most suppliers offer courses on their products but training on their work practices and management techniques will be less available. If the supplier is unable to supply one the training is best done on the job with the supplier's staff. The agreement to do this should form part of the contract. Other methods of learning about the supplier are listed in Chapter A10.

PERSONNEL REQUIREMENTS

The people required to perform the work necessary for the staffing and training of the customer's project teams are the team members themselves and specially designated members of the customer's personnel department. Normally the project manager will be first appointed and then he will arrange for the appointment of those reporting to him (either current staff, contract staff, or recruited staff). These individuals will then arrange for the appointment of those reporting to them, etc. The ideal situation may under the pressure of timescales be somewhat truncated, but it should be noted prior to contract even for the largest projects the teams will have a maximum of three management strata apart from the support administrative/clerical staff.

APPENDIX: PERSONNEL CLASSIFICATIONS

These personnel classifications will be common to both the customer's project team and operational system support (maintenance) personnel and the supplier's development personnel. However, the difference in attitude between development and support personnel should be noted.

The classifications, of necessity, are broad, covering a wide spectrum of job skills at all levels in the organizational hierarchy. The members of the project teams will tend to be at the more senior levels, and they should therefore have the ability to designate the type of person required at the more junior levels.

USER

The 'user' is anyone who will actually utilize the system as part of their work or other activity. It also applies to management responsible for those staff. However, care should be taken to differentiate between those who are active users (or performing the above function daily), and those who work only in areas connected with the user discipline (i.e. planning), although they were once active users.

Examples of active users are:

1. A member of the public using a cashcard machine.
2. An air traffic controller using a computerized radar screen.
3. Clerical staff using an invoicing or accounting system.

COMPUTER

The computer knowlegeble person is one who is more concerned with the design, programming, and subsequent software support and operation of the system, than the application itself. Job titles within the overall computer person title include system designer, systems analyst, system tester, application programmer, systems programmer, operator, data controller, data processor etc.

At the levels of system designer the computer person will be extremely intelligent yet relatively inexperienced compared to other professions. He will have a tendency to see everything in logical computer terms. The computer person will use his high intelligence to offset his relative lack of experience, but his colleagues from other disciplines must make him aware of things he might miss.

ENGINEER

The engineer in computer projects falls into two categories. The electronics engineer who is concerned with the intricacies of the computer and communications system, and who can integrate various pieces of computer and communications equipment, diagnose faults, perform routine maintenance, etc. The electrical engineer with certain mechanical engineering skills who is responsible for power supplies, environmental systems and loadings on computer room floors, etc. Quite often both the necessary skills will lie within the abilities of one person.

The engineer will be highly skilled, competent and practical. There is always the possibility of friction with his computer colleagues with relative salaries often a factor in this.

MANAGER

The manager is responsible for making a group of people work together as a balanced team, under him, to achieve things within previously estimated timescales and budgets.

The manager will be conversant with management techniques for costing, estimating and monitoring money and timescales and, most importantly, know and be able to execute the management of people. Junior and middle management must have sufficient technical knowledge to differentiate between technical truth and fiction; match ability, training and experience to tasks and foresee the pitfalls that might occur.

Generally it is very difficult to find a manager who is sufficiently competent both managerially and technically. The manager, by his very position, may be a political animal and it is important to select one whose political game playing is limited to that necessary to advance the project rather than his own ambitions. If he is doing the latter he will be wasting time and energy to the detriment of the project.

ADMINISTRATOR

A person who operates or supervises a procedure so that it operates efficiently and expeditiously and who tries to ensure the procedure is used whenever applicable. Whatever his level there may be a tendency to conservatism which will conflict with the changes that computerization will bring.

LEGAL

In this book's context, a person who can devise contractual conditions to meet corporate/project requirements or who can interpret contract conditions as to their impact on organizations and projects.

His work necessitates a pessimistic outlook which is vital should something go catastrophically wrong with a project. However, this attitude could be a brake on positive thinking.

ACCOUNTANT

One who can monitor and analyse the finances of a project/organization, devise financial means of meeting organizational objectives and assess the financial implications for a project/organization.

His work necessitates an outlook which is unsympathetic to anything that cannot be quantified and to that extent again he may be a brake on positive thinking. As with the legal person, however, his advice must be taken into account in the decision-making process.

CHAPTER A4

FEASIBILITY REPORT

Once a customer organization has the idea of using a computer to provide certain facilities, it is necessary for the organization to provide resources to study the idea. The study should provide answers to the following questions:

1. Is the project feasible?
2. Can it be justified?

The answers to these questions will be contained in a feasibility report which should be the outcome of the study.

Large organizations may possess a formal system for requesting (an operational requirement request—Chapter D1) and handling feasibility studies. This should ensure that requests will come from a manager with sufficient seniority to ensure that adequate resources are committed to the examination.

The examination can be undertaken by an operational analyst(s) specializing in the type of application concerned. However, this is a rare skill and it is more common for the work to be undertaken by someone or a team with considerable knowledge of the application (i.e. a user) or by a computer expert(s) (who should be experienced) termed a systems analyst, who acquires some knowledge of the application. The criteria for deciding which method to adopt are more often the result of organizational structures and politics rather than more sensibly the personnel available and the complexity of the application. Hitherto the former method has been used for the more complex real time system, i.e. systems which function at the speed and within the timescale of the application, and the latter for commercial data processing systems.

For the large, very complex application a multi-discipline team is required and it is important that it is a team in a true sense not divided by professional or organizational loyalties. Location of the team should therefore be in one place, preferably in an open-plan office. Quite often the inspiration for the project will have come from the computer side; however, it is important that from an early stage the user department is seen to be taking an active role. Ideally the users should be the driving force. It is important also that at least one of the team is an active user. This probably means he will require some computer training.

Where the project, because of its size, cannot justify a team and can only support one or two people it is important that the missing knowledge is obtained by effective communication with the appropriate experts. Variations on the team versus individual approaches can be used including brainstorming (where a multi-discipline team totally concentrates on a topic behind closed doors), but the important thing is to ensure that all relevant knowledge (as described in the Personnel Requirements section of this chapter) is gathered, synthesized and presented.

The question of feasibility will be ascertained in several ways:

1. Is the proven technology necessary to perform the task commercially available?
2. Does the organisation possess or have access to the necessary resources including finance to provide a solution?
3. Will the solution fit in with the organization's environment, and in particular will its staff be prepared to use it?

The project can be justified in several ways:

1. The requirement cannot be met without a computer.
2. Significant financial/staff savings can be achieved over the life of the system. Beware! This is the most commonly used justification and the savings anticipated have seldom been achieved for a variety of reasons.
3. Staff cannot be found who will tolerate manual methods because of the required low skill level; social stigma, etc. However, be careful not to justify a system because it is fashionable.

If after several iterations round the loop of possible solutions, scope of the automation, feasibility and justification a conclusion is arrived at, a short feasibility report (see Chapter D2) should be issued. Alternatively, if after the expenditure of the resources set aside for the study no conclusion is arrived at, the senior manager should be requested to provide more resources. If he is not willing to provide more resources the conclusions to date should be made the topic of a short report which can be used for future reference.

PERSONNEL REQUIREMENTS

The personnel contributing to the feasibility study are those given below with the qualities listed.

USERS

1. Recent operational knowledge.
2. Some computer knowledge including similar projects.
3. Organisational knowledge and analytical ability.
4. Technical writing ability.

COMPUTER

1. System design analysis.
2. Technical writing ability.
3. Application knowledge.

ACCOUNTANT

Corporate financial knowledge.

The designated team leader will require management skills.

CHAPTER A5

OPERATIONAL REQUIREMENT SPECIFICATION

If the feasibility report recommends the project should go ahead and a corporate agreement is obtained a steering committee, as described in Chapter A1, should be set up. This committee should set up functional, timescale, and financial objectives for the production of an operational requirement specification. It will also see that the team that produced the feasibility report is augmented sufficiently to perform the larger task of producing the operational requirement specification. However, as shown in the Personnel Requirements section of this chapter, it will encompass a similar set of experience and skills.

In order to foster the team spirit and overcome organizational/discipline boundaries it would help the project if the team were housed in an open-plan office where an unrestricted dialogue can take place.

The operational requirement specification is a vital part of the project. Its objectives are:

1. To communicate in some detail what the eventual system will do.
2. To 'freeze' the project's, objectives at a realistic level and enable the minds of all connected with the project to be concentrated.
3. To form the basis of a document which can be issued to suppliers as defining what should be tendered for.

The document will contain for convenience a copy of the feasibility report. The document will be written principally in user jargon with a glossary of terms. Computer jargon should be avoided wherever possible. This will reflect the document's purpose which is to say what should be done and not how it is to be done.

Within the document will be described all functions that the system has to perform. For the purposes of tendering and implementing, all functions should be designated as being mandatory requirements; desirable requirements, or simply nice ideas.

The document should specify the maximum load the system should carry under all conditions of use, including fallback mode (and, if applicable, training and test modes) in addition to the main operational mode. In fallback mode the system functions with a reduced capability because a failure, etc. is preventing full normal service.

The maximum load is a function of the specified relative frequency of the various input message types from the various originating devices, allowing for specified percentages of messages to be entered correctly and incorrectly. For every transaction, the average and maximum input and output data (e.g. number of characters in a message) should be stated. The worst case message entry should also be specified and how the system should perform if it is exceeded. The maximum rate of all transactions for the hour peak load and for the short-term (say ten minutes) peak during the peak hour should be stated. The minimum response times allowed for each mode's maximum load for the short-term peak during the peak hours should also be specified. These should be expressed as a percentage tolerance, e.g. 95 per cent of all responses will be within two seconds. Response times are usually defined as time from pressing the input key for the input message to first character of the relevant output message. This definition is operationally useless if there is a significant delay before the second character is output. A more sensible definition would be to the last character of a meaningful element of the output message. 'Meaningful' could be qualified as the first record visual display unit (VDU) line, or some other valid character string.

The operational requirement specification will quantitively state how reliable the system should be, what the availability requirement is, etc. Within the operational requirement specification there is a need to specify all rules, procedures, algorithms, that the system will use. All error possibilities should be described with the resultant action, including error messages specified.

It is advisable that the analysis of the requirement is carried out using a structured analysis methodology. The benefits of this are:

1. The analysis of the operational requirement is broken down into more manageable elements, thus aiding estimating and progressing of the analysis task.
2. Using a proven method saves time reinventing the wheel and the time-to-competence of new staff can be much shortened by training.
3. The methodical and systematic approach a structured technique imposes reduces the risk of omissions and ambiguities and improves communication between all those involved with the requirement.
4. The structured approach eases the task of modification and maintenance of both the requirement and the system to meet it.

Structured approaches are based on the division between data and processing and their interrelationship. The use of a structured analysis methodology is strongly recommended.

Several structured methodologies are available ranging from those based on simple relationships of data and processing to more rigorous mathematical techniques involving rigorous proving of the specification.

It is *vital* that the operational requirement is as comprehensive and unambiguous as possible. Clarity is vital. To ensure this it should be validated by a third party or parties examining the implications of every twist and turn in the logic of the text ('walking through'). A checklist of the contents of an operational requirement specificationcontents is given in Chapter D3.

Aside from the operational requirement specification itself the team will establish budgetary resource estimates and timescales for the completion of the project.

Large organizations will have a formal system for the document layout, production referencing, distribution and approval of operational requirements. Whether or not a formal system is used, the approval should be given by the manager or steering committee, who should be of sufficient seniority positively to commit all the necessary resources required for the implementation of the system and its subsequent operation.

Upon approval the operational requirement specification should come under configuration management (see Chapter C1).

During the production of the operational requirement specification the team will have to consider several questions and utilize certain techniques, namely:

1. Large computer systems take several years to become operational and a careful attempt must be made to predict what will be the operational requirement when the system is predicted to go operational.

2. For very large, complex or innovative requirements, an advanced version of the operational requirement specification could be released as a discussion document for suppliers. Although care has to be taken to strip the feedback of its sales and marketing wrappings this can yield valuable information. This is particularly so if budgetary estimates are requested. These can be vital when assessing financial feasibility.

3. It is important for the team to decide what is a sensible grouping of the application facilities to automate. Factors that will affect this decision include:
   (a) A minimum number of involvements with other applications functions.
   (b) The upper limits of what is manageable. The constraint of organizational politics should be included here.
   (c) The logical grouping of functions.
   (d) The collection and processing of common data.
   (e) Finance available. For this the team will require occasional inputs from the financial department of the organization.

4. The work of the team would be greatly facilitated if a prototype of the system could be constructed and exposed to eventual users. A cheaper method would be a 'paper prototype' where users specify their 'causing' actions and the logic is 'walked through' on paper and the users are presented with the effects verbally.

5. The use of emulators and/or simulators could prove beneficial in trying out features proposed for the operational system. Although expensive, if an organization is likely to implement a number of projects, investment in a general emulator or simulator, the cost of which could be spread over several projects, might be sensible. The technique could involve a general purpose computer on which crude approximations of different scenarios of a possible operational system could be put together (i.e. simplify functions, do not attempt to tune performance). Specimen active users could then be invited to assess the various scenarios in a controlled manner and their attitudes recorded and analysed. Apart from the practical value of such techniques, the effect on the operational acceptability of the final system, if the user feels he has had his say, should not be underestimated.

The operational requirement should be presented to the steering committee for approval together with any revisions thought necessary to the project's objectives.

PERSONNEL REQUIREMENTS

The personnel contributing to the operational requirement are as given below with the qualities listed.

USER

1. Recent operational knowledge.
2. Some computer knowledge including similar projects.
3. Organizational knowledge and analytical ability.
4. Technical writing ability.

COMPUTER

1. System design/analysis.
2. Technical writing ability.
3. Application knowledge.

At least one user and/or computer person should be knowledgeable in the structured analysis technique to be used.

ACCOUNTANT

Corporate financial knowledge.

The designated team leader will require management skills.

CHAPTER A6

INVITATION TO TENDER

Before work on the invitations to tender commences it is assumed that the following conditions apply.

1. The steering committee has given approval for the implementation of the system as specified in the optional requirement specification described in the previous chapter. Also the project objectives have been reset.
2. Funding for the capital and life costs will be available. These will have been ascertained as part of the feasibility study. The project team should update the funding requirements to include an allowance for inflation and reasonable contingency, if this has not already been done.
3. For this purpose of the book's scenario the decision has been taken to meet this requirement by going to suppliers for a turnkey system. If this route is not intended the user department should still read on as a significant proportion of this chapter will still apply to alternative scenarios.
4. A customer project team is set up, constituted as described in the Personnel Requirements section of this chapter. Wherever possible it will have continuity with the project team that produced the operational requirements specification.

The first stage in the invitation to tender is the taking of certain key strategic decisions viz:

1. Will the customer go out to contract first for a functional specification and design (as described in Chapters A9 and B7) followed by an implementation contract? If this is to be the approach several points require consideration.
   (a) Are suppliers awarded a functional specification and design contract to be permitted to bid for the subsequent implementation contract?
   (b) Will two or more functional specifications and design contracts be awarded and the best of these be used as the implementation approach?
   (c) Will the winner or winners of functional specification and design contracts be expected to bear some of the costs of the work

37

themselves? This will be some of the amount they otherwise would have to spend on sales effort bidding for an implementation contract.

If separate functional specification and design contracts are let, care should be taken to see that they do not build in feature which would make implementation harder.

2. Is it likely that there will be a requirement to have an update of the functional capability of the system, after acceptance from the supplier and before going operational, as suggested in Chapters A10 and A12? This will almost certainly be the case with projects having long implementation timescales. If it is deemed one should be required, time and money must be made available for it. Care must be taken to see that this phase, if included, does not become a catch-all with decisions not being faced, and work being deferred from earlier phases in the belief it can be done then. It may be necessary for this reason, not to broadcast the possibility that such a phase may be included and the prospect simply kept in the minds of senior management.

3. Is maintenance on hardware and/or software to be performed by the supplier or a third party, or done in-house?

4. Will the supplier operate the system or will customer's staff? If so who will undertake their training? Generally if one has a training department and/or a large number of people to be trained, one method is for the supplier to train a number of the customer's instructors.

5. Will the system, after acceptance, remain functionally static? This will mean that updates of manufacturers standard software may not be required. However, beware! The author has never seen a system which stayed functionally static under pressure of users requirements. A decision must be made on whether the contractor is to be given a free hand with the design, or whether some degree of design is to be done in-house. Beware of the danger of over-constraining the supplier.

6. A decision must also be made on the projected life of the system. This is important because a decision has to be taken as to the level of technology which is required from the system. If the latest technology is used there is a risk and cost associated with pioneering. If older technology is used there is a different risk and cost associated with operating and maintaining obsolete equipment, which could be the case towards the end of the project.

7. Once this framework has been laid down, consideration has to be given from whom to invite tenders. Some organizations in the public sector will have no option but to advertise publicly for tenders because they are bound by national or trade community (e.g. EEC) rules. However, advertising for tenders is also valid if one has little knowledge of the market place or if one is pioneering a new application. Advertising for suppliers should be placed in the computer press. If overseas tenders are required, use can be made of the appropriate

international publications, but the closing date for applications for invitations to tender should be advanced for at least two weeks. If the result is a large number of requests for invitations to tender, a first pass can be made to reduce the number by requesting the potential tenderers to submit a short (ten pages) proposal. This short proposal can concentrate on the tenderers corporate viability (financial standing, size, etc.); track record; available staff numbers, as well as the more technical matters. The responses should be sufficient to reduce the number of tenders to four to six. This makes a sufficient number to give a spread of technical solutions and prices while not overloading the customers team with too many tenders to evaluate.

If the customer is confident and can select his tenders without the long listing process described, the following criteria should be used in addition.

1. Always select the market leader.
2. Always select the most prestigious supplier. He may be the same as 1. Although he may not offer a cost effective solution his offering could act as a yardstick against which others can be judged.
3. Select suppliers who have satisfactorily performed for you in the past.
4. Select any supplier who in his sales and marketing has shown a particular enthusiasm for your business.
5. Beware manufacturers, unless purchasing standard products alone. Their range of computers may not be suitable for your application, generally they are multinationals and their domestic operation may only be a sales arm with limited or no technical support capability, particularly no application software department. They do however generally, have lots of resources worldwide and access to hardware at cost price (important if performance becomes a problem).
6. Beware suppliers that are over committed either in a personnel (particularly software) or a financial sense. A rough guideline is that a contracts value at any point in time should not exceed 10 per cent of their business at that time.
7. Beware software or systems houses which are generally financially weak and understaffed on engineering. This is particularly so if your project has a large portion of its work in communications.

The latter three points do not necessarily preclude these types of supplier, but the dangers should be noted.

Ideally the short list should comprise the market leader, the prestige company and two companies that have special attributes like novelty of approach, special interest in the project etc. If one is unsure of the approach to be adopted, e.g. a minicomputer or a mainframe computer solution, then choose two of each type in a short list of four.

Once the short list has been established the full invitations to tender will be prepared and sent out. They will comprise the following,

TENDERING PROCEDURES

This will contain the request for proposals and details of closing dates, opportunities for inspection, discussions and presentation, format and content of tenders, contact points, performance bond requirements (if applicable), etc.

OPERATIONAL REQUIREMENTS

This will be essentially the operational requirements specification as described in chapter A5. It should be prefaced by a general description and history of the application and specifically how it functions inside the tendering organization. Also it should include a glossary of terms. If results from a prototype or simulation exercise exist, these too should be included.

TECHNICAL REQUIREMENT

This will list the technical details required in proposals, it should detail the points of the organization's general computer policy. (e.g. we only use IBM computers, or we wish all new software to be written in ADA). Also if not covered in the operational requirements the physical constraints of where the system is to be located should be precisely described (with engineering drawings where appropriate). The relevant installations standard should also be reformed and supplied (see Chapters B9 and D10)?. Other details such as the availability of existing computer for use operationally or for software development/maintenance should be mentioned. The requirements for future development (hence initial flexibility) and maintenance of the system should be chronicled with details of any constraints. An appreciation of the likely job skill and aptitudes of personnel that will be associated with the system should be included. If any benchmark testing is required this should be indicated here.

It may be avoidable, but some areas of specification will inevitably be vague and ambiguous. Some customers do this deliberately so that changes in specification can be forced on the supplier at a later day. This may be possible but it is not worth the risk of all the contractual argument that will ensue. Genuine areas of uncertainty should be cleared, identified and marked for later discussion.

IMPLEMENTATION STRATEGY

This will list the implementation requirements particularly timescales. The supplier should be asked to give his implementation strategy (see Chapter B8) with milestones, team number and organization. Although it will be generally difficult for the supplier to do, at tender stage, some names and career details of possible key members should be requested. The supplier should also give his design (see Chapter B7), documentation (see Chapter

B14); test (see Chapter B10) and quality assurance (see Chapter B13); plans or standards on these should be specified to him in documents accompanying the invitation to tender.

N.B. It is best for the supplier to undertake the project using his own standards provided they meet the customers requirements. Working or conversion to an alien format could introduce errors and will certainly cost more.

Any miscellaneous requirements should be included, such as documentation having to be prepared on a wordprocessor and, if possible on one compatible with a type in general use within the customers organisation.

CONTRACTUAL REQUIREMENTS

The customer should include his requirements for the contract to supply the system as specified. He should do this by attaching a draft contract to the invitation to tender with a request that the supplier include in his proposal a contractual compliance statement in addition to technical compliance statement.

The invitation to tender should state the type of price that should be quoted (cost plus, fixed, etc.). An indication of the level to which the price should be broken down, should be included. This should allow some elaboration to permit the suppliers commercial considerations to emerge, e.g. cost of money discounting; marking up, etc, also the cost of individual facilities. The purpose of breaking the price down is to allow 'adjusted' prices to be calculated (because 'like' is never 'like') and cost-value to be ascertained (see Chapter A7). Fairer comparisons between rival tenders are thus made much easier. Sufficient information should be requested so that the life costs of the system can be calculated, as a system with a 10-year life will have maintenance costs which are likely to exceed the capital cost of the system. A stage payment plan could be suggested but the supplier will normally prefer to discuss this during the pre-contract negotiations (see Chapter A8). Because prices are commercially sensitive they should not be included in the main body of the proposal, they should be included in a covering letter, which will have a more limited circulation. Better still they should be requested in a sealed envelope, separate from the invitation to tender, so that they can be opened *after* the technical evaluation of tenders is complete.

A more comprehensive checklist for the invitation to tender is given in Chapter D4. When the invitation to tender has been prepared and possibly approved by the steering committee it should be distributed simultaneously to all suppliers on the short list. All suppliers should be given opportunities for inspection, discussion and presentation. The closing date for tenders should allow adequate time for sensible proposals to be made. (What is decided at this time gets set in contractual concrete and can make or mar a project.) Two months should be allowed for a major system. Extensions to a closing date should only be granted in extreme circumstances but it would

42

be shortsighted to rule out an excellent proposal because the delivery van broke down, etc. The suggested format for the proposal shown in Chapter D8 will simplify the comparison process during tender evaluation.

PERSONNEL REQUIREMENTS

The customer's personnel contributing to the preparation of the Invitation to Tender are as given below with the listed qualities:

USER

1. Recent operational knowledge including the operational requirement.
2. Some computer knowledge.
3. Organizational knowledge.

COMPUTER

1. General.
2. Tender preparation.

ACCOUNTANT

1. Some computer knowledge.
2. Knowledge of computer industry financial/commercial practices.

LEGAL

1. Contract law.
2. Some computer knowledge.

ENGINEERING

1. General.
2. Significant computer knowledge.

ADMINISTRATOR

Document control expertise.

The designated team leader will require technical editing ability in addition to management skills. All team members will have ability to communicate intelligently in both verbal and written form.

CHAPTER A7
TENDER EVALUATION

All tenders which are to be considered, should be passed over to the evaluation team immediately after the closing date has passed. Ineligible tenders for reasons of unjustified late delivery or unsolicited tenders, etc., should be returned to the appropriate suppliers with a letter of explanation.

The objective of the evaluation will be to place the tenders in the order in which they most meet the customer's total requirements and rule out tenders that are unacceptable. The total requirement covers functional, technical, commercial and financial considerations.

The evaluation team will consist of individuals possessing the mix of experience shown in the Personnel Requirements section of this chapter. Again continuity with the team preparing the invitation to tender is highly desirable. However, it is highly unlikely than an evaluation team drawn from within the customer's organization will be able to provide expertise across the board for all tenders from within its own experience. The use of consultants could provide a possible solution.

Inevitably the onus of evaluation will mostly fall on the computer personnel within the team. Apart from not having the necessary span of knowledge, these individuals will undoubtedly be biased towards particular companies, makes of computer and design solutions. This bias can in fact be in either direction namely the 'not invented here' and 'the grass is greener on the other side' syndromes. The point is of particular significance if an existing computer system is being replaced or the client already has a number of computer systems. It is vital that all members of the evaluation team clear their minds, before the evaluation, of any idea as to whom they should choose. Although this is difficult to do, unless it is attempted the whole process becomes a costly exercise in wish-fulfilment.

The evaluation team should have started work before the tenders were received. During that period they should have compiled comprehensive lists of questions on all aspects of the required system—operational, technical and financial. Chapter D6 lists possible questions for choosing the supplier. These questions should have been weighted in relation to each other. A question and hence a weighting should be included for each required facility. Certain questions should have been designated as critical. In this context 'critical' would mean that failure of any tender to meet the necessary criteria on that facility would make the whole tender invalid. Obviously these questions would carry the highest weighting and would be based on mandatory features in the invitation to tender. Mandatory feature however, should be chosen so as not to rule out all possible solutions. The cost evaluation should be carried out by assessing the life costs of each offering, using the same technique for all. The bidding suppliers should be encouraged to make positive commitments on their future pricing policy for items such as changes and maintenance.

The complete list of questions should be applied to each tender and an appropriate numbered mark given for each question. Where a tender fails to answer a question is should be given zero marks and this should only be altered if during subsequent questioning (if this occurs) the bidding supplier gives an answer with satisfactory data. Where suppliers offer facilities not in the invitation to tender they should be given a mark and the facility a weighting. The weightings should be applied to the marks and the total weighted marks for each tender calculated. The tender with the highest weighted marks and no failures on critical questions should be deemed to be the one that most meets the customer's requirements in total. If price is particularly sensitive the financial corrections should be subtracted. A table of non-financial weighted marks against life costs can then be established, ignoring tenders with critical question failures. A value judgement can then be applied. Simplistic solutions, like taking the cheapest should be avoided. More sophisticated approaches like 'cost-value' can be utilized. Here the comparative life costs per weighted mark can be calculated for combinations of mandatory, desirable, nice and supplier-suggested facilities and a supplier chosen using the relevant criteria.

The evaluation, however, is again futile if it is based solely on data presented by the bidding suppliers in their tenders and during any presentation that they might make. There is no substitute for the evaluation team being able to verify the facts presented to them.

Some techniques for verifying tenders are:

1. Introduce consultants into the evaluation team—they should have a wider knowledge of the industry, but bear in mind that they can exhibit the same tendency to being biased as customer staff.
2. Talk to existing customers of the bidders. Be aware, however, that they may be reluctant to give facts which could show they made a mistake in their choice of supplier.
3. Consult other avenues such as the computer press, the industry grapevine and user groups (organizations composed of customers of the same supplier for the exchange of information and lobbying the supplier).
4. Talking, off the record, to members or ex-members of the bidding suppliers staff can also yield fruitful information.
5. Requesting a 'benchmark' (calibrated performance test) and running

it on configurations (hardware and software) as near as possible to those proposed by the suppliers.

6. Inspect the supplier's premises and see if his claims are backed up (e.g. evidence of staff levels). The running of the benchmark should also be observed. It is advisable to prepare a checklist of points before the visit.

These points are not as helpful when it comes to the special-to-project elements of the tender. Here it is simply a matter of checking that the supplier says he will meet the requirement without any obvious caveats and trusting that, aware of the contractual ammunition at the customer's disposal, he will implement his promises. The only possible guide is the supplier's previous record and the current availability to the supplier of the staff who were responsible for the success stories in that record.

It is quite possible that the bidding supplier will offer a standard package to meet all or part of the software element of the requirement. This should be checked line by line against the operational requirement. The technical compliance statment should help here. Because standard packages tend to use a lot of computer power, performance should especially be examined. Assuming the package provides all the mandatory requirements, it should be evaluated on a price basis against the cost of writing special-to-project software which should meet all the requirements. The case for using a package will be improved if it already has a number of users whose unibiased personnel can confirm the supplier's claims. This will generally rule out a lot of existing software. Considerable scepticism should be shown towards packages and existing software particularly if they originate from a single user requirement.

Presentations can be useful as a means of assessing the objectivity of the proposals, but only if the supplier has his presentation given by the technical members of his team (with if possible those who are going to be on the implementation team) and restricted in length so that well-prepared questioning can take place.

It is of crucial importance to the success of the project that one should meet the key members of the bidding supplier's implementation team, particularly the project and software managers. This is so important that it could in extreme circumstances override the evaluation decision if it has not been made part of it. The right people with the right track record are often more important than the supplier that employs them. It is also important that there will be no unreasonable delay to the project caused by an excessive time for the supplier to set up his team.

Care should be taken with all tenders to check that promises made by the supplier's sales and marketing function are substantiated by his production function.

The tender evaluation process should be carried out in secret. This is not only to be equally fair to all suppliers bidding and avoid undue influence but to avoid the impossible situation for the evaluation team that would result if they were barraged with the constant stream of tender revisions that would result from contractors learning things as the evaluation proceeded. Generally there is no reason why the bidders should not be told the names of the competition. They will inevitably have found this out using their own knowledge of the market and the grapevine.

Before proceeding to inform their management of the decision, the evaluation team will check that the feasibility study is still valid, particularly in the area of cost. If not, a fresh feasibility study should be made based on the tenders. If this comes out negative the project should be reviewed and probably discontinued.

The results of the evaluation should be a detailed report containing recommendations to the steering committee. They should overturn the project team's recommendations if they are severly flawed or there is an overriding policy reason for so doing. They should never be overturned because of approaches made to the steering committee by one of the competing suppliers.

PERSONNEL REQUIREMENTS

The evaluation team should include: those given below with the qualities listed.

USERS

1. Recent operational knowledge including the operational requirement.
2. Some computer knowledge.
3. Organisational knowledge.

COMPUTER

1. General including many manufacturers, companies and contacts in the industry as possible.
2. Ability to be objective and ignore personal prejudices.

ACCOUNTANT

1. Knowledge of computer companies commercial policies.
2. Knowledge of corporate practices and costs.

CHAPTER A8

PRE-CONTRACT NEGOTIATIONS

Once the evaluation team has made its selection and it has been approved by the steering committee, the chosen supplier should be invited to the customer's pre-contract negotiations. The other suppliers should be advised of this, but not in a manner that would prevent the reopening of negotiations with them if the negotiations with the first-choice supplier break down.

It is possible that the unsuccessful suppliers will attempt to come back and revise their proposal, probably in the price area. It is then the customer's decision as to whether these late revisions should be considered. However, if they are, the following should occur:

1. All the tenderers should be invited to do the same thing.
2. A full revision of the evaluation process should take place.

However, all this will consume time which will affect the overall time-scales of the project and evaluation team effort. This effort may cost more than the value of the offered revision. Also questions must be asked of the company making the revision, as to whether they had either made errors in the original estimation of the project (which poses questions against their competence) or, more likely, they are now for commercial reasons offering to do the job for an uneconomic price. This would not be a satisfactory position as there would always be financial pressure on them to implement in a less than satisfactory way, or renegotiate the contract price at a later date.

The customer's objectives during the pre-contract negotiations should be to clear up the inevitable misunderstandings that will have occurred during the tender process. Also, although the chosen supplier is the nearest to meeting the customer's total requirements, he may still be some way from meeting it completely. Even though this is normally very difficult it may be possible during pre-contract negotiations to move the chosen supplier's tender closer to the customer's requirement.

The pre-contract negotiations on the customer's side will be handled by the senior members of the evaluation team reinforced—unless they have the necessary authority—by one or more of the steering committee. Wherever possible, however, the evaluation team should have the necessary authority.

Where technical issues are at stake subcommittees can be set up and these may involve the more junior members of the evaluation team.

The misunderstandings which occur during the tender process could include all the facets of the requirement—operational, technical, implementation, strategy and financial. Inevitably the possibility will have to be considered that these misunderstandings could prove to be so great that the evaluation of the contractor has to be reassessed. This could result in a new first choice, in which case pre-contract negotiations should be started with him. This should be very carefully handled. It is possible that those responsible for the production of the operational requirement and the invitation to tender may be psychologically unable to admit to ambiguities and omissions in their documents, and in this case going to a 'not the first choice' supplier may simply perpetuate the same problem. Generally a supplier who says that there are no problems with these documents should be viewed with suspicion. All this takes time and any decisions taken must always bear in mind the inevitable impact on the overall project timescales. However, decisions taken to proceed along an unsatisfactory course purely in the interests of preserving the current timescales will inevitably lead to delays because of the greater difficulty of rectifying changes once a significant part of the work has been completed.

The process of making the chosen supplier's offering closer to the customer's requirements is difficult. Again it may not be possible to move the supplier to a position where his tender may satisfactorily meet the requirement. This again may result in a new first choice and the second-choice supplier being approached. However, it is probable that even after modifications of his offer he may be less able than the original first choice to move towards an offer which may satisfactorily meet the requirement. Consideration should therefore be given to abandoning the project in its current form.

The customer may not only want to move the chosen supplier's offer closer to his original invitation to tender but also may wish it to include changes he has thought of during the interim. These may indeed be ideas from the other suppliers' tenders, subject to any copyrights being infringed. Care should be taken that changes introduced in this manner do not negate the whole tender process although this, in reality, is the only opportunity before acceptance that this process can be contemplated.

It is important for the customer to realize that, until the contract is signed, he has the power of the competitive situation over the supplier. Pre-contract negotiations therefore represent realistically the final opportunity for the client to ensure that the supplier is proceeding in a way that will meet the required technical timescale and contractual objectives.

One major item to be resolved on the pre-contract negotiations is agreement on a stage payment plan. From a customer viewpoint all stage payments should be set against measurable achievement milestones and *not* the projected dates of those milestones. This will effectively mean that there is a built-in penalty clause system for delay. Because of this there is a tendency for customers to weight the payments profile towards the later stages of the project. However, this will generally mean an increased price when the contractor adds interest costs. Whether this is acceptable involves calculations concerning interest rates, projected inflation rates, etc. Whatever is decided upon, it is prudent (and accepted commercial practice) for up to 15 per cent of the contract price to be retained for a period after successful completion of the project.

It is possible that customer and supplier may have different costs of money. The supplier will have an 'opportunity cost' of using the money to further his business. Where possible this should be discussed and the position of equal advantage to both sides established.

Assuming that a stage has been reached between customer and supplier where all but minor misunderstandings have been ironed out, a set of baseline documents can be agreed upon. A baseline is a consistent set of system elements which give a known functional capability. These will consist of invitation to tender, supplier's tender (suitably amended by the pre-contract negotiations) and subsequent correspondence. However, this will be super-seded by a functional specification document (see Chapter A9) which will be jointly drawn up and agreed by customer and supplier.
. The baseline documents will then include this functional specification and where it conflicts with other documents in the baseline its wording will apply.

Normally the production of a functional specification document will be the first milestone in a contract with the chosen suplier. With large and/or complex projects the project may be divided up into two or more contracts, the first of which is for the production of a functional specification document.

Normally the supplier who wins this contract would be expected to, at least, perform the next one.

However, assuming the functional specification document is not the subject of a separate contract, once the pre-contract negotiations are successfully completed with the chosen supplier, the losing suppliers should be informed of the situation. Where possible, they should be briefed on why they lost the contract on the understanding that no discussion will be entered into. This will make for a better competition next time round, which is to the customer's benefit. After this point no consideration for the losing suppliers should enter the customer's thinking.

PERSONNEL REQUIREMENTS

The personnel involved in the pre-contract negotiations are: the evaluation team (with possibly a member of the steering committee), except the Administrator who nevertheless will support the negotiations by producing and controlling the documentation and documentation changes emanating from the discussions.

CHAPTER A9

FUNCTIONAL SPECIFICATION

After contract signature, the next major milestone should be the completion of the functional specification.

The functional specification document is *vital* to the success of the project. It has the following objectives:

1. The supplier's involvement in the production of the document helps to make his staff fully aware of the operational requirements of the system.
2. The customer's involvement in the production of the document helps him fully to understand what the supplier is offering in terms of operational facilities and the overall system concept which will provide these facilities.
3. The involvement of both customer and supplier in its compilation makes both parties more committed to meeting the system objectives described within the document.
4. The document will serve as a communication medium between the user and those employed on the development of the system.
5. The document will serve as an educational tool for both customer's and client's personnel who require an overall understanding of the system. This will include personnel joining both project teams, senior management of both the customer and the supplier and the eventual users of the system.
6. The document will serve as a basis for writing the Acceptance Tests.

The document will be produced by the supplier's project team but with heavy involvement of the customer's personnel particularly in agreement to its contents in total.

The functional specification will particularize all functions which the system must perform and will necessarily include functions not mentioned in the operational requirement.

Also unlike the operational requirement, which just specifies the behaviour of the system as seen by the user, the functional specification will specify how this behaviour is to be accomplished. The document will thus be a composite of the operational requirement and the supplier's tender.

The functional specification will contain all the information in the customer's operational requirement specification minus the feasibility section. It will reflect the changes agreed during the pre-contract negotiations.

Additional to the above, the functional specification will contain an overview of the system design that will provide the operational facilities. This will include all major hardware and software (both package and special-to-project) elements, their interconnections and the computer language(s) chosen. Details of design standards will also be contained within the document. User and computer jargon will be avoided wherever possible but, in any case, the document will contain a comprehensive glossary of terms. The document's contents are shown in Chapter D7.

The analysis will be conducted using the structured analysis methodology used in the preparation of the operational requirement. The designs should be done using a structured design methodology compatible with the structured analysis methodology.

The specification should be validated for completeness and unambiguity by third parties from both customer and supplier.

The responsibility for the timely preparation of the document will lie with the supplier and particularly his project manager. However, he will normally request the customer to nominate personnel within the customer's organization, who will be responsible for answering questions and giving approval to the relevant sections. The final document will also require approval. The customer must be prepared to do this and provide the answers to questions, comments on drafts of the document and finally approval, in an expeditious and timely manner if he is not to be cited by the supplier as a reason for delay.

Once agreed the document will form the basis of configuration control (see Chapter C1).

It should be noted that project planning will have been carried on in parallel with the production of the functional specification.

PERSONNEL REQUIREMENTS

This will require the evaluation team although the loadings on individuals will be somewhat different. The accountancy and legal input is not normally necessary at this stage.

CHAPTER A10

SUPPLIER MONITORING

This chapter strictly deals with an implementation which has been put out to a supplier. However, several of the topics covered apply to implementation by a computer department, particularly if that department has a high degree of autonomy. Supplier monitoring commences once the contract has been signed.

We must first be aware of the purpose of supplier monitoring. It is to ensure that all is proceeding correctly with the work being performed by the supplier, and that any clarifications and changes to the specification are correctly and expeditiously handled. If this is not found to be the case, measures can be taken, in conjunction with the supplier, to correct the situation, or, if this is not possible, to take timely measures to minimize the impact of the problems caused. If no supplier monitoring was undertaken, in all probability the client would only learn of failure or slippage upon acceptance date, far too late to correct the situation or minimize the impact.

At all times those monitoring a contract must ask themselves the question 'Is the sum total of their client organization's objectives more likely to be met by continuing with the contract or cancelling it?' If an honest appraisal leads them to the latter conclusion it should then be cancelled. The contract should make provision for this. The decision should always be taken by the steering committee on the advice of the project manager and his team. The criteria for making this appraisal can sometimes be made on a financial basis. However, quite often intangibles like staff morale or public image enter the equation, making the appraisal more difficult, but nevertheless it must still be made.

Additional to supplier monitoring the customer's personnel can be involved by participating in walk throughs (see Chapter B8), etc.

The supplier monitoring will be conducted by a team embodying the job skills shown in the Personnel Requirements section of this chapter. The team will have some continuity with the evaluation team, but will grow in size as there is an increase in the supplier's work requiring monitoring. This build-up should lead to the team that will eventually operate and support the system. If there is to be a change in the customer's project manager this is the time for it to happen. The newcomer can be more objective about the supplier and his performance than the one responsible for the selection of the supplier.

Once a contract has been signed, the customer has inevitably lost some degree of control over the project. Up to that time (assuming a competitive position) the supplier will normally go along with all but the most unreasonable demands of the customer. However, once a contract has been signed, apart from the delaying of stage payments, the only other way in which a customer can regain control of the situation, if say the supplier has behaved totally unresponsibly, is by recourse to the contract and particularly any punitive (such as penalty) clauses contained therein. This is simply admitting that the object of the exercise—a system meeting the requirements which will become operational in the requisite timescale and cost envelope—has not been achieved. Even the secondary objective of obtaining redress may not be met because there is no such thing as a watertight contract.

A computer contract, like any other contract, ensures that both sides are aware of their responsibility, ensures adequate insurance against injury, etc. However, it may also provide the customer with a deterrent to ineffectual performance by the supplier. It is important that supplier monitoring is conducted so that it does not, in any way, weaken the deterrent powers of the contract. Some of the more important reasons/excuses given for non-fulfilment of the specified requirement, timescale and budgeting overruns are:

1. *Changes to the specification.* The customer can ensure that these are not made an excuse by asking the supplier to give the timescale and budgetary impacts of reviewing the proposed changes, in addition to the normal request for the timescales and budgetary impacts of implementing the changes. Most prudent suppliers will insist on this anyway. Even if this safeguard is included the monitoring team would be well advised to ensure that the supplier gets the absolute minimum number of change proposals to consider.

   This particularly applies to the stages between agreement on the functional specification and system acceptance. Chapter B8 describes fully the problems the supplier will encounter if his team is expected to evaluate changes let alone implement them, while working to a budget and a timescale on the implementation of what was the agreed functional specification and design. Customers who find it essential to change the specification are well advised to withhold their change requests from the supplier and, after reviewing them together, group them into a total package of changes. They should only present this package to the supplier during the final stages of his system implementation. They can then form the basis of a second version of the system as suggested in Chapter A12.

   The customer should also restrict his personnel, particularly those working with the supplier's team, from discussing informal ideas in such a way that the supplier's personnel might construe them as change requests. One further way of reducing the impact of changes is formally (by the change control procedures) to see that they are used as offsets for waivers in the specification that the customer might well ask for.

2. *Specification Ambiguities and Greater Implementation Difficulty*. If the supplier was only committed to giving a fixed price after the agreement on a functional specification (see Chapter A9), except in extreme circumstances the supplier has no good reason for using these as reasons for non-performance. However, if the supplier was forced to go fixed price before the functional specification was agreed he may well have a reasonable case. It should be noted that in the course of tendering and then preparing the functional specification the supplier will have done a considerable amount of design work, certainly sufficient to alert him to significant ambiguities and the level of complexity.

3. *Provision of management information for supplier monitoring*. It is quite possible that the supplier will use the alleged extra effort required in providing this information as an excuse for non-performance. This is not reasonable. The supplier should have this information readily available if he is really managing the implementation. The customer can avoid giving cause to this excuse if he simply plugs into the supplier's own project control mechanisms. Copies of the project plan, discrepancy reports, etc. should automatically go to all members of the monitoring team, thus reducing considerably the supplier's time spent in answering questions. The monitoring staff should have access to all tests and test material (see Chapter B10). This method of working should be stressed on all members of the customer's organization. Resources and times should have been formally agreed within the contract for handling any remaining queries.

4. *Delay or non-performance of customer actions*. Even with a turnkey project the customer will have to perform certain actions by certain dates if the supplier is to perform satisfactorily. It is obviously vital that the customer not only performs these actions by the agreed dates for the success of the project but also so that he does not provide the supplier with an excuse for non-performance. The actions can cover a variety of circumstances, e.g. the provision of power supplies, information, agreement to documents, tests, etc.

Additional to finding reasons for non-performance, the supplier may formally request a relaxation of his contractual obligations in the form of waivers. Apart from trading waivers off for extra supplier commitment elsewhere in the project, the customer should not totally reject waivers out of hand. It will not profit the customer or his project if the supplier finds the project becoming commercially unacceptable. However, the customer's prime objective of the supply of a system with the full specified capability in a timely manner must be paramount in his considerations.

Apart from the plugging in to the supplier's management procedures, the customer's main means of monitoring the supplier's implementation will be the progress meeting. This will be held at intervals no greater than a month and should be chaired by a senior member of the client's organization. It should have a formal agenda and use the project plan as an *aide-mémoire*. It should not debate technical issues, but should delegate them to a sub-committee of those particularly concerned. Actions agreed at the progress meeting should be carefully recorded in the minutes of the meetings to ensure they are carried out. A great deal of ambiguity and non-productive conversation will be avoided at progress meetings if these actions are numbered and referred to by their numbers.

Normally the function of quality assurance (see Chapter B13) is given to the supplier. A member of the customer's supplier monitoring team should be given the responsibility of seeing it is being carried out correctly.

Finally, although the customer's control over the contractor is reduced, in another important respect he is in a much better position after contract signature. By virtue of the lower working level relationship he becomes much more aware of the contractor's true ability rather than the image the sales department has created. However, the techniques for researching the supplier used in tender evaluation (Chapter A7) are still useful. User groups in particular help inform the customer of details he needs to consider when he takes over responsibility for the system.

PERSONNEL REQUIREMENTS

The customer's monitoring of the supplier requires a similar mix of job skills and disciplines as that required for tender evaluation, with the following exceptions:

Accountant

Only required when changes or stage payments are being discussed or considered.

Legal

Only required if the legal aspects of the contract are being discussed or considered.

Note the progress of testing scripting and testing will be happening in parallel (see Chapter A11). Those customer personnel involved should be considered part of the team.

CHAPTER A11
TESTING

The involvement of the customer with testing commences soon after contract signature and is carried on in parallel with supplier monitoring. The purpose of testing in general is to prove that elements of the system work in accordance with the functional specification; and that these elements as they are integrated with other elements to form larger elements still work in accordance with the functional specification. This process is repeated until the total system is assembled and thus works in accordance with the complete functional specification. Acceptance testing has the purpose of demonstrating to the customer's satisfaction that the system works in accordance with the functional specification.

Chapters B10 and B12 contain details on how testing and acceptance testing should be carried out. This chapter confines itself to the work the customer must carry out, to see that testing and acceptance testing are performed satisfactorily. The work will divide itself into an observing function and possibly a participatory function.

The observing function will be performed by members of the customer's project team as outlined in the Personnel Requirements section at the end of this chapter.

The first involvement is in the agreement of a joint test plan. This should contain for the customer's benefit details of his involvement in the testing process, particularly in the accpetance tests required, although strictly these should only be an amplification of points covered in the main contract.

The plan should be agreed early in the life of the project for three reasons:

1. It is more likely that this will be in the 'honeymoon' phase of the project and hence it will be much easier to reach agreement.
2. The preparation of test scripts and anticipated results can be as time consuming as the production of the actual system, therefore the sooner this work is commenced the better.
3. It will enable the adequacy of the functional specification to be checked our before problems caused by deficiencies in the functional specification become serious.

The customer's test observing should check that the supplier's test team is as independent as possible of the supplier's implementation teams. The customer's test observing should also check that, because of the problems of overcoming deficiencies in the testing of the supplier's standard products, that all major units are tested prior to acceptance. Because most customers will insist on these major units becoming his property upon the relevant stage payment, this testing being done successfully will be a prerequisite of payment. If it fits into a sensible test programme it is advisable also to do this for hardware when items are delivered to the customer's premises. Thus defects that could have been caused by damage during transit are checked.

The customer's test observing will also be responsible for checking that the acceptance tests are carried out satisfactorily. They may be aided in this by customer's personnel participating in the test function (see below). Acceptance testing should be carried out independently of normal testing. Where possible it should be conducted in an operational environment. The process is important, for in addition to its prime objective, it gives the supplier a goal to aim at and thus concentrates his collective mind. The senior customer personnel will be required to be observers of acceptance tests.

The customer's participatory testing personnel will actually work on applications testing with the supplier's test team, for this demanding task they will require training in the intended tools and methodologies.

This participation is required because when it comes to the application areas it is probable that only the customer will have sufficient personnel with the necessary knowledge of the application to write test scripts and predicted results scenarios. However, the presence of customer personnel in the supplier's organization can cause problems, in particular in giving the contractor reasons for delay and increased cost. Customer personnel working in this area must therefore be carefully briefed. Specifically their tasks must be to raise test scripts and result scenarios on the system as specified and not their own personal views of it. (The difficulty of users doing this can be appreciated, but it is vital that they do.) Furthermore, their question-asking and knowledge-gaining must take place through channels that are contractually allowed for.

Normally the test team will report to the supplier's project manager. This will present problems in the areas of standard hardware, firmware and software where the project manager is obviously under great pressure not to criticize his company's production line offerings. The customer's personnel participating in testing must be prepared to raise discrepancy reports (see Chapter C2) against standard products, even if they do not conduct tests on them. The methods of finding what bugs are present in standard products (e.g. membership of user groups) are described in Chapter A7.

It should be noted that for satisfactory testing quite often a full, or possibly a representative operational database (or more mundane files), requires setting up. A representative database will contain at least one of each record type, feature, etc. specified in the functional specification. Ideally it should contain data gathered from the real operational situation, but recourse to simulated data may sometimes be necessary. This task is again sensibly performed by the customer's personnel participating in the testing. However, again, it can provide an excuse for the supplier to put the blame for test failures on this database. The only way to overcome this is to agree criteria for the comprehensiveness of the database within the test plan and to make sure that these criteria are met.

It should be noted that in certain cases the volume and nature of the data may be such as to justify a large data preparation and verification facility.

When acceptance testing is complete an acceptance test report should be produced describing the results of the acceptance testing and recommending whether the system should go operational or not. This should go via the project manager to the steering committee.

PERSONNEL REQUIREMENTS

The customer's personnel involved in observing the testing will be those members of the team performing the main supplier monitoring. However, the customer's personnel participating in the testing will normally be junior to, and reporting to, the main monitoring team. They will have the following qualities:

USERS

1. Detailed knowledge and understanding of the functional specification.
2. Some computer knowledge, particularly of test tools.
3. Attentive to detail.

COMPUTER

1. General computer knowledge.
2. Particular systems knowledge, specifically performance analysis and support tools.
3. System testing experience.
4. Attentive to detail.

ENGINEERS

1. Some applications knowledge.
2. General engineering knowledge.
3. Ability to use hardware diagnostic tools.
4. General computer knowledge.
5. General applications knowledge.
6. Attentive to detail.

CHAPTER A12
GOING OPERATIONAL

Once the system has passed all its acceptance tests with a positive acceptance test report it is then a candidate for going operational, assuming all the conditions specified in Chapter D13 are met. One important condition is that there is a sufficiency of trained staff available to use, operate and support the system as specified in the Personnel Requirements section at the end of this chapter. Figure A3.2 shows a possible organizational structure with the exception of the day-to-day users.

Another important condition is that, where required, a complete operational database must be tested and ready for use before the system is used operationally. The size of the task of preparing a database should not be underestimated, although it will, of course, vary considerably according to the nature of the customer's business. Database preparation should begin as early in the project as possible, particularly if computers had not previously been used. Information collecting is likely to be a time-consuming pursuit and the data preparation team must have the opportunity to gain experience before the system goes operational.

Where there is a very large amount of data to be collected and/or complex checking of it is required, a computer system for this may be necessary. This should be procured with sufficient lead time so that the main project is not delayed.

Before the system goes operational, there is one danger. Although the users who specified the system had current operational knowledge and a close dialogue was kept up with the future actual users during the life of the project, the passage of time could well mean that the original operational requirement which the system performs could be different from the current operational requirement. The system should therefore be designed from the onset for ease of change, with a modular structure and no built-in parameters.

However, I would not recommend a relaxation of the stated attitude to change notes during implementation to overcome this problem. Changes written during the life of the project may themselves require changing upon acceptance and indeed in some cases require reversion to the original specification. Furthermore, changes written against a working system have a larger probability of being operationally satisfactory rather than those written against an abstract concept like an operational requirement.

If this situation appears at all possible at the start of the project, resources and timescales should be set aside for an update of the system between acceptance and the system going operational. This could be handled under a contract extension or the opportunity could be taken of blooding the customer's teams (if they are planned and/or exist). In this latter case it would probably be prudent to have a hand-holding contract for some of the supplier's experienced people to be part of the activity so that this expertise is transferred. Whatever approach is adopted, all changes must be handled under configuration management using the change control procedure (see Chapter C1).

Consideration should be given during the planning of the project to a period of parallel running between the old methods and the new system. Often this will not be practical and inevitably it can be expensive. Certainly if it is adopted the period should be severely restricted as it can give users the time to enter into a never-never attitude about the new system. A better approach is to phase the introduction of a new system. This phasing can be done by introducing one group of users to the system at a time and is attractive in that it spreads the training and possibly the peripheral installation workload. Another method of phasing is the introduction of system functions in groups. This eases the learning step the users have to go through. However, it is dependent on how the split between new system functions and old system functions, operating together, can be handled.

A modification of this approach would be to introduce the new system for a fixed limited period, e.g. one day, after which the old method of working would be reverted to, regardless of the performance of the new system. The results could be analysed at leisure and other, possibly longer, trial runs could be staged until it has been decided that the next successful trial will be kept running permanently.

Whatever method is employed for introducing a new system it is highly desirable that the point or points at which responsibility is transferred from supplier to customer are clearly identifiable and have been specified at contract signature. When the system has been operational for some time and is stable, it is sensible to carry out a post-implementation review. This should check the original assumptions, particularly the feasibility of the system, and how they compare with the original results.

The information gained should be used as a basis for improving the forecasting on future applications.

The actual decisions on the above should be taken by the steering committee based on written advice and plans submitted by the project manager and his team.

The steering committee should then, say at the end of the warranty period or when the system is reported to be stable, whichever is the later, set a date for the system's disbandment. This will be upon their acceptance of the post project review (see Chapter D14). The responsibility for the system then becomes a line management function.

PERSONNEL REQUIREMENTS

The customer's monitoring team members will still be heavily involved up to and after the system going operational, apart from their possible roles in the operational support organization. They will be doing such tasks as conducting the post-implementation review, organizing maintenance contracts, etc. The other requirements will be for personnel both operating and supporting the system as given under the headings below.

USERS

Actual users, who have been trained in the use of the system, performing their operational function using the system.

Other users performing management, training, planning, etc. roles in relation to the actual users.

These personnel will mainly not be in the system support organization but will be in user or service departments.

COMPUTER

Computer operations staff including operators, media librarians, managers and specialist skills such as database managers, network and communications managers, etc.

Software maintenance and development staff depending on the cut-over in responsibility from supplier to customer.

OTHER

The system support departments will make use of service departments (e.g. accountancy, legal, personnel) in the same way as any other department in the organization.

CHAPTER A13

WARRANTY AND MAINTENANCE

The purpose of warranty is to reassure the customer that, although the system passed its acceptance test, any problems which will inevitably show up during the early operational life of the system will be corrected by the supplier. Both the hardware and software that are supplied with a turnkey computer system contract should be supplied with warranty. The normal period for this warranty is 12 months and is normally geared to the final stage payment of a retained sum which normally represents up to 15 per cent of the capital value of the contract. Warranty will not normally cover preventative maintenance, and will therefore be concerned with the supplier's action to overcome unforeseen problems. The warranty should contractually specify the maximum time in which the supplier must respond to (not fix) faults, and the totality of the cover. This totality can vary between working hours, Monday to Friday or continuous—24 hours a day, 7 days a week.

Many suppliers offer different classes of service with cover and response times being the differences between them. The higher the service the greater the price, and though it is generally within the overall turnkey price, the customer should positively decide his real requirements in this respect. It should also be noted that hardware and software may require different classes of service.

Customers should be careful in the understanding of what warranty consists of: the supplier will normally supply warranty subject to a preventative maintenance contract being taken out. This is reasonable as obviously the supplier cannot give warranty guarantees unless he is sure the system is being maintained and he has knowledge of this maintenance. However, a contractual phrase like '12 months' warranty will be supplied subject to a maintenance agreement being taken out' could mean that effectively no warranty is being provided, the correction of faults after acceptance is simply covered by the maintenance contract. This will cover both preventative and fault-fixing maintenance and unless a price is agreed at turnkey contract signature, it can leave the customer vulnerable. Ideally during the warranty period only a hardware preventative maintenance contract is required, all faults, both hardware and software, being corrected under warranty.

Normally all significant design and specification faults will show up during the warranty period and this is fine unless the customer is going to provide his own maintenance, particularly for software. Then he will want his own staff to work in parallel with the suppliers and this will present problems in placing the responsibility for remedial action and cost impacts. This is normally overcome by having a support contract up to a level which the customer considers sufficient for his needs and no warranty agreement as such. Care must be taken to see that there is continuity of personnel between the customer's project team and this support.

The supplier will also need a policy on the application of updates to the supplier's standard software. Updates may necessitate a lengthy conversion of data, application code changes and could introduce new errors. If there is definitely no requirement to vary the functionality of the system, it may be possible to avoid taking any updates. This is seldom the case. Nevertheless, the customer will usually want to reduce changes to a minimum while the system is settling in, which may conflict with the supplier's wish to introduce updates to clear faults under warranty. Also, as a general rule, unless some offsetting factor is present (e.g. significant price discount) their implementation should be delayed until other customers have had experience of them. User groups can provide this information.

Maintenance is the term that covers all activities aimed at keeping the system's hardware and software problem-free (planned maintenance) or necessary to fix problems once they have arisen (unplanned maintenance). All maintenance should take place under configuration management.

The customer must make decisions as to whether he wishes to perform his own maintenance. It is advisable that hardware maintenance both planned and unplanned is handled by the same organization. However, separate decisions can be taken for hardware and software. Should a situation be reached where different elements in a system are maintained by different manufacturers, an arbiter is required for faults which cannot be directly assigned to an element. This arbiter may be one of the customer's personnel or the prime maintenance supplier.

Generally a customer should not do his own hardware maintenance unless he has sufficient units of the same equipment:

1. To make self-maintenance, and the necessary spares holding, cost effective;
2. To ensure that his staff are proficient in fixing faults, because of a sufficient frequency of exposure to them.

If a customer decides not to do his own hardware maintenance, he should consider independent maintenance organizations as well as the supplier or the equipment manufacturer. The effect of any leasing agreements on hardware maintenance strategy should also be considered.

The customer's decision as to whether to perform his own in-house software maintenance is dependent once again on the level of changes to be applied to the system and the existence of (or the cost of setting up) an in-house software department. The reluctance of programmers to do purely maintenance work should be a consideration in the decision. Chapter B16 describes the difficulties suppliers will have in providing maintenance (and indeed warranty) cover for special-to-project software. Scepticism should be shown to supplier's claims for this unless he puts a price on it which shows he appreciates his problems. However, he may have a maintenance department for special-to-project software, but this should include mechanisms for the project team passing on their knowledge to this department.

One final factor which should be considered in the maintenance strategy to be adopted for both hardware and software. This is the confidentiality of the application and hence who should have access to it. This could prevent any form of external maintenance.

There are several methods of performing hardware maintenance. Two which can be used by customer or supplier are:

1. The customer or supplier carries a large spares holding on site and has staff capable of effecting diagnoses and then replacement of parts from complete units (e.g. disc drives) down to cards. These are then sent away for repair.
2. All maintenance is done on site which has the staff and equipment to repair below card level. This reduces the spares holding but the provision of a workshop may be required.

In the case of the supplier performing the maintenance, his staff will normally visit the customer's premises although critical or large applications may require a permanent presence on the customer's site. This will of course cost the customer more. Thought should also be given to the timing of planned maintenance. Normally time is allocated during the lean period in operational activity. However, this has a cost implication. Whatever time is allocated should be contractually agreed once the equipment has been handed over from supplier to customer.

Some system designs may have very high resilience features. These, in the way they permit the system to tolerate failed units or permit maintenance while operations continue, could affect the way maintenance both planned and unplanned is performed, and must therefore be considered.

Software maintenance will be conducted by the applying of source corrections in a system build–system test–system build sequence as used during system implementation (Chapter B8). However, if changes are being simultaneously added, sufficient priority should be given to the maintenance fixes so that the changes are always applied against a stable system version. This will include new standard software releases.

All maintenance should be carried out under configuration management. Maintaining under configuration management means that except in extreme circumstances, the full range of relevant testing is conducted before the system is released for operational use. This should be done even if only one line of software is altered. The use of patches (temporary software fixes) should also be under configuration management, although they should be avoided wherever possible, and limited to a low maximum number that can be present in the system at any one time.

Whatever the maintenance arrangements, the operational user should be provided with a single point of contact to inform if the system malfunctions. Where all maintenance is provided externally, this should be the prime contractor, who, if the system is large enough, may have a continuous or part-time presence at the customer's premises.

There are two charging methods offered by maintenance organizations. The first is a scale of fixed charges for the level of cover provided. Level of cover means, for instance, on site, two-hour response available round the clock, weekends, working hours only, etc. The second is a charge varying according to the amount of support requested. The prudent approach is that for the first years of maintenance, the customer opts for the fixed level charge appropriate to the criticality of his operation. During these years he establishes his actual maintenance requirements and can determine whether the second method will be more cost effective. If it is he can then adopt it.

Should the customer perform his own maintenance he still should feed back problems and change requests to the supplier or manufacturer. Only if this is done will the development of standard products be influenced by customers.

The general pattern of maintenance requirements is for hardware initially to show a large number of problems (teething), then to settle down to a long period with a minimal number of problems, and then as it wears out the number starts to increase. This reaches a point where it becomes cheaper to replace it. Software after the initial (often large) number of teething problems, never wears out. The major maintenance task is keeping up with the updates to manufacturers' standard software and changing all software to cope with a situation which it has not encountered before and for which it was not originally written.

PERSONNEL REQUIREMENTS

The personnel requirements for the maintenance of the system are as follows. The actual day-to-day users of the system are not referenced because they could require a variety of skills and expertise dependent on the application. If the maintenance is totally contracted out, only the user element will be required. However, customer's liaison personnel will be required between the operational users and the maintenance organization whatever maintenance arrangements exist. The personnel requirements for the complete maintenance of the system by the customer are as follows:

USER

1. Current operational knowledge.
2. General technical knowledge of the installed system.

3. Ability to communicate.
4. Knowledge of the configuration management procedures.

COMPUTER

1. Programming and testing ability in the language and techniques of the installed system.
2. Knowledge of the system.
3. Knowledge of the configuration management procedures.

ENGINEERING

1. Technical skills/ability to diagnose faults in and maintain the computer and communications equipment comprising the system.
2. Knowledge of the configuration management procedures.

MANAGEMENT

1. General knowledge of the operation.
2. General knowledge of the system software/hardware and communications.
3. Management ability.
4. Knowledge of the configuration management procedures.

CHAPTER A14

SYSTEM RETIREMENT

Inevitably there will come a time when the retirement and probable replacement of a computer system has to be considered. Those involved in taking this decision will possess the shop skills shown in the Personnel Requirements section at the end of the chapter.

The replacement of the system will follow the processes described in this book; however, the customer organization should be in a much better position because of the experience gained with the original system to specify the requirements for its replacements. However, additional thought will have to be given in the requirement to the method by which one switches from the original to the new system while offering the users a tolerable level of services.

There are four reasons why a new system should be contemplated:

1. The old system hardware is proving difficult and costly to maintain.
2. The old system software and data structures have been modified so many times that further changes are proving difficult and costly and the incidence of bugs is reaching intolerable levels.
3. It is proving increasingly difficult to find staff within the organization who are knowledgeable about the system and/or who are sufficiently motivated to provide the necessary support services (inevitably, staff will want to work on up-to-date equipment).
4. The system has become overloaded and this cannot be accommodated by a simple upgrade.

The criteria for deciding when it is time to move on to a new system will vary with organizations. With some, operational effectiveness will be all important, with others the decision will be simply financial. Whatever the reason, the decision to retire a system must be taken with sufficient lead time to allow a new system to go operational before the stability of the system being replaced becomes critical. The person charged with the timely raising of the issue of system retirement will be the manager in charge of the support organization.

It may not always be necessary to replace the complete system. Sometimes a change in hardware may be all that is required, conversely new software may be introduced on existing hardware. A phased replacement will have the advantage generally of a less risky replacement path and a more even demand on resources.

PERSONNEL REQUIREMENTS

The personnel contributing to the decision to retire the system are those given below with the qualities listed.

USER

1. Knowledge of the existing system.
2. Knowledge of future operational requirements.

COMPUTER

1. General computer knowledge, particularly state of the art.
2. Knowledge of the existing system.

ENGINEERING

1. General engineering knowledge particularly the current state of the art.
2. Knowledge of the existing system hardware.

ACCOUNTANT

1. General accounting knowledge.
2. Knowledge of the cash elements involved in running the existing system.
3. General corporate financial knowledge.

SECTION B
SUPPLIER ACTIVITIES

CHAPTER B1

FINANCIAL/COMMERCIAL CONSIDERATIONS

It is predicted that the market for turnkey computer systems will increase significantly. This trend will be coupled with a relative decline in the role of customers' own computer departments. Generally it will be advantageous for suppliers to enter this growing market. They should be aware of the high cost of bidding for a turnkey. This cost must be considered along with the project risks and chances of getting the contract before it is decided to tender. These suppliers will fall into three basic types—computer manufacturers, systems houses and major companies with high electronics interest. Each of these types will tend to have fundamental strengths and weaknesses in the turnkey market-place. While capitalizing on their strengths they must overcome their weaknesses or hide them from their customers.

COMPUTER MANUFACTURERS

These companies start with the following advantages:

1. They make up to 100 per cent profit on their hardware, over their production line costs, with which they can subsidize their special-to-project software.
2. They are often large multinational companies and thus can afford to rescue ailing projects, if they so desire, with extra funding.

However, they quite often have problems with turnkey projects in countries other than those where their prime manufacturing facilities (including standard software) are located. This is because their subsidiaries in these countries are set up as primarily sales organizations with technical staff supporting the sales function. This type of organization often has difficulty in finding staff to man project teams and reorientating them to manage and produce the special-to-project software in turnkey systems.

SYSTEMS HOUSES

These companies start with the following advantages:

1. They are staffed by large numbers of software people with wide experience of turnkey systems and the different applications and types of software involved.
2. They do not have to use the equipment from one manufacturer but can choose the equipment best suited to the project. (NB. This is only an advantage if they can allocate to the project, staff with the necessary experience of that equipment.)

Systems houses generally have the following disadvantages:

1. They have difficulty in competing on price with the computer manufacturers, because although they get OEM discounts on hardware of up to 35 per cent they often mark this up by 15 per cent, and even if they do not, they are uncompetitive with manufacturers' production costs.
2. Quite often they can have the problem of under-capitalisation, so that they are put at a disadvantage if cost of money (interest on borrowed capital) becomes a factor. This not only applies to the new small systems house but even to older-established systems houses, which may even have become subsidiaries of large companies.
3. Systems houses are often weak on hardware (computing and communications) engineering resources. This, however, is not always as bad as their traditional engineering customers might perceive.

MAJOR COMPANIES

These companies have the following advantages:

1. They are far better equipped to handle projects which have more facets than simply computing.
2. They have the resources, like manufacturers, to rescue ailing projects with extra funding, if they so desire.

Major companies can, however, have the following disadvantages:

1. They may carry significant overheads, which tends to make them more expensive than say, system houses.
2. They do not always retain the best software personnel. This is because they can only pay salaries pegged to the electronics industry norms. These do not take account of the marketability of skilled software personnel.

To offset the various weaknesses of different supplier types, various combinations of companies may get together for a particular tendering situation. Examples could be for a large computer/communications turnkey, a systems house and a communications equipment manufacturer bid as a partnership. For a multi-faceted turnkey, a major electronics company acts as prime supplier with a systems house as computer system or software subcontractor. The dominating criteria for determining the nature of the partnership and the roles the companies play in it are normally what are the capital value, added value and/or risk-carrying ratios between the partners.

Turnkey computing contracts are a relatively new feature and the market shows a surprising volatility. Because of the difficulty of estimating (particularly software costs), suppliers tend to underbid their first tenders in a particular market-place. Once having won a contract and then lost money on it, they then tend to go the other way and become expensive. Because of the underbidding of new suppliers, more experienced suppliers are tempted to go in for loss leading. There are two ways to recoup the loss.

1. By utilizing as much of the software as possible in a quasi-package for fresh orders in the same market-place. Although someday this approach may pay off, experience shows the benefits of this approach to be largely illusory.

2. By recouping the loss using significantly larger than is commercially normal mark-ups on extensions to the initial contract or even by renegotiating the contract, price beyond the point of no return in the project life. This process has occurred not only by design but when inexperienced suppliers have found themselves in trouble when they have won a contract with an underbid. Experience shows the supplier nearly always gets away with it. One of the reasons for this is that the customer manager responsible, once he has chosen his supplier, is a hostage to fortune through his inability to admit his mistake by cancelling the contract. The renegotiation situation can also be brought about by customer action. However, this is less likely if the procedures for change control and the production of a functional specification, as suggested in this book, are adhered to.

Several detailed commercial issues need to be considered by suppliers: viz:

1. Quite often the customer may find it attractive or even demand that the domestically manufactured content of any system is maximized. This may extend in a case of an overseas tender to a partnership with one of the customer's indigenous suppliers.

2. It is probable that the customer in a tendering situation will set great store by the quality of the supplier's staff presented to him (see Chapter A7). The supplier should give serious consideration to having his 'best' people in sales support as opposed to implementation teams. There is some legitimacy in him doing this, for the initial creative design work involved in a tender requires different skills from the slogging attention to detail of implementation.

Despite the difficulties, the expanding market ensures that customers are not short of potential suppliers, nor suppliers short of potential customers.

CHAPTER B2
STAFFING

The supplier will normally set up a project team to design and implement, etc. a system to meet the customer's requirements. Many of the activities involved in the staffing of the team (e.g. recruitment) are almost identical to the customer's staffing activities and definitions as described in Chapter A3. It should be noted that generally a supplier can offer a computer person wider experience and better promotion chances in the computer profession than a customer can. The impact of this varies with organizations and projects; however, it can affect customer/supplier relationships. Certainly no staff 'poaching' should take place during the contract phase.

A supplier's project team will have the structure, including the key positions which are now described.

The person directly charged with meeting the customer's requirements will be the supplier project manager. While he/she will be conversant with the technical issues of the project, he/she should be more aware of staff management techniques and the use of the project management techniques of Section C. He/she will have an attitude that meeting timescales is more important than technical niceties. His/her duties will keep him in daily contact with the customer and it is important that a rapport is established and preserved as far as possible. To this end, he/she will report to a manager who, amonge his/her other duties, will have that of ensuring the project is profitable for the supplier and who will therefore take up more potentially acrimonious issues with the customer. In general, in medium or large companies this manager will oversee several projects/contracts in the same way.

The project manager will have reporting to him/her the technical management for the project. This will normally comprise a software manager, an engineering manager (on most projects one engineer may suffice) and a test manager. The software manager, depending on personalities and size of project, may or may not be the chief designer. Also reporting to the project manager will be an administrative manager (again on most projects one person may suffice). Additional to the normal administrative duties he will be responsible for updating the project plan, etc., running the system to allocate computer time and keeping the financial bookkeeping for the project's budget. Most customers who are aware of quality assurance will have requested that the quality assurance manager is independent of the project team. This will present no problem to large suppliers which have a quality (or standards or inspection) department. However, in small suppliers' organizations he might well report to the project manager's manager.

There will be several positions on the larger teams which will justify junior management status. Among these are the person responsible for system builds, who will report to the manager of the test team. Also, if there is no general support and development facility, this function must be catered for within the team. Generally, in this limited environment, this will be headed up by a junior manager who should report to the engineering manager within whose remit the equipment on which the facility is provided lies. One danger that should be avoided here is that of an engineering manager to whom the equipment becomes an end in itself, resulting for example in him giving priority to maintenance rather than the service the equipment should provide. One further possible position for a junior manager is that in charge of support software within the software team. However, on very large projects this could be combined with the support and development facilities manager's position to form a support manager's position reporting directly to the project manager. A junior management position of technical editor may also be required if justified by the level of documentation.

The rest of the project team will report to the line managers under the project manager. Generally the software team will be by far the largest. If concepts like the IBM chief programmer team are followed there will be computer librarian positions within the software teams which will reduce the administrative function. If customer's personnel are to be used they will generally report to the test manager, although there may be a few in the design teams undergoing on-the-job training. A typical team structure is shown in Figure B2.1.

The teams will build up during the early days of the project. It is important that this build-up is not too sudden or else the whole team can become bogged down in training and/or familiarization. However, it should not be so gradual that time-scales are impacted.

It is important that there is some staff continuity from the bid team, although the changes that occur should make the team lean more towards achievement rather than conceptual nicety. If the project is a long one, some staff turnover is inevitable, and in some respects desirable, so that a freshness is maintained. A question of balance is required and attempts by the customer to achieve total stability should be resisted for this reason.

Although customers may object, the use of carefully selected contract staff may be a means of filling gaps in the team or injecting specialist expertise which is only required for a short time. If this option is taken they should be understudied as far as possible and thus made more cost effective.

The supplier's project team will be greatly assisted if there is some user knowledge input into the work. One way this can be introduced is by employing someone from the user discipline and deploying him/her on the project via the quality assurance function.

76

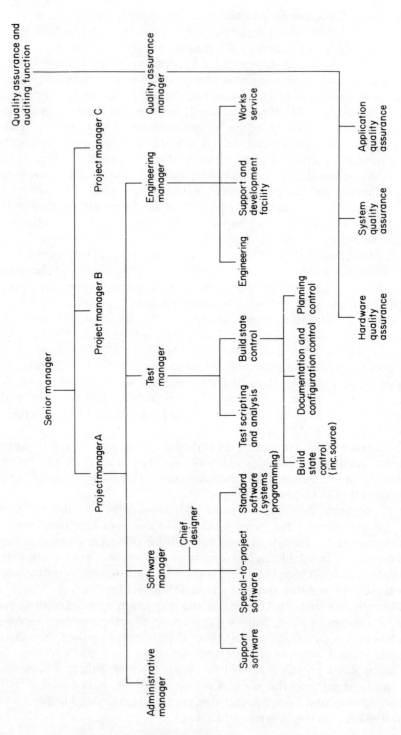

Figure B2.1 Suppliers Project Team—Possible Structure

PERSONNEL REQUIREMENTS

The supplier's project team management are given below with their required qualities listed.

PROJECT MANAGER'S MANAGER

1. Commercial acumen.
2. Knowledge of company.
3. General computer knowledge.

PROJECT MANAGER

1. Extensive management skills.
2. Some knowledge of company.
3. General computer knowledge.
4. General engineering knowledge.
5. Some application knowledge.

SOFTWARE MANAGER/CHIEF DESIGNER (JOB MAY BE SPLIT)

1. Significant management skills.
2. Significant application knowledge.
3. Considerable computer knowledge.
4. Significant engineering knowledge.

ENGINEERING MANAGER

1. Some application knowledge.
2. General engineering knowledge.
3. Significant computer and communications knowledge.
4. Management skills if he has an extensive team working for him.

TEST MANAGER

1. Management skills.
2. Significant application knowledge.
3. Some computer and communications knowledge.
4. Considerable computer system testing knowledge.

ADMINISTRATION MANAGER

1. Management skills.
2. General company knowledge.
3. Administrative skills.
4. Project management mechanisms knowledge.

Support manager (job may be split into junior management posts.
Support and development facility manager and support software manager)

1. Management skills.
2. General computer knowledge.
3. Particular computer operations knowledge.

All more junior staff will require appropriate mixes of the above skills with one or two specialist ones (e.g. database designer as appropriate).

APPENDIX: PERSONNEL CLASSIFICATIONS

These are the same as those covered in Chapter A3 apart from those unique to the supplier side, namely:

MARKETING

One with general knowledge of the industry who can foresee future trends and can see sales opportunities and possibilities for new products. Generally an amiable far-sighted realist with enthusiasm for his particular industry.

SALES

One who can convert sales opportunities into orders. Although ideally he should have a deep understanding of both applications and computing he may become, almost of necessity, a broad-brush individual thinking primarily in the short term.

CHAPTER B3

MARKETING AND SALES

Before a customer/supplier relationship is established it is necessary for both parties to be aware of each other to the extent that:

1. The customer recognizes the supplier as an organization that can meet his requirements; and
2. The supplier recognizes the customer as an organization whose requirement he can meet in a way that directly or indirectly increases his profitability.

The establishment of this relationship is the general role of marketing. The turning of this relationship into a firm order from the customer to the supplier is the function of sales.

Marketing in a turnkey computer system context includes market research, advertising, publicity, sales promotion, etc. Specifically important in turnkey situations is the development of a long-term relationship with the customer, which is not only of direct sales benefit but allows the supplier to influence the customer's requirement in such a way that it enhances the probability that he will get the eventual contract. Sometimes, particularly with systems houses, this comes not through a marketing relationship as such but in the supplier doing consultancy work which is a prelude to a turnkey contract.

The exact demarcation point between marketing and sales is often quite difficult to determine. Because of this, and also to preserve the continuity of personal relationships with the customer, the marketing and sales functions can be merged. Even if they are not, the functions of both marketing and sales include the tasks of representing the supplier to the customer and the customer to the supplier.

Where the implementation is being done by a computer department which is internal to the customer, this department will still have to 'sell' its services to the rest of the customer's organization. Corporate policy may even dictate that the computer department competes with external suppliers.

It is usual to consider that marketing and sales have only the single function of obtaining business for their company and serve no other purpose in meeting the project's objectives. However, given that decisions taken early in the life of a project are critical, and that initially marketing and sales are generally the only contact between client and tendering supplier, it is fair to assume that the marketing and sales function is in a position to make a vital input. This assumes that the marketing/sales person involved has a sufficient knowledge of the application and technical details of his company's products and/or abilities. Additionally the marketing/sales function will be responsible, in the early stages of the procurement prior to the invitation to tender, for the briefing of the supplier's technical personnel on the requirement; and the more perfectly that occurs the better the solution. To do this satisfactorily he must ascertain what is in the customer's mind. This need not necessarily coincide with what is in the invitation to tender.

Also the marketeer's/salesman's appreciation of the budget available for the project can have a considerable impact on what is offered. What is of equal importance is getting an indication of such facts as who are the customer's key decision-makers, etc. which, though of vital importance to the marketing/sales effort, are less important to the general meeting of the operational requirement.

This document will not comment further on the techniques of marketing and sales which are not specific to computer systems. However, it should be noted that in the turnkey situation, marketing and sales personnel with significant knowledge of the application are vital. Even if they have considerable application and technical knowledge, a significant amount of sales support will be required.

PERSONNEL REQUIREMENTS

Marketing/sales personnel with the qualities listed below.

1. Significant applications knowledge.
2. Significant computer knowledge.
3. Significant engineering knowledge.
4. Considerable applications and computer industry knowledge.
5. Considerable marketing and sales experience and ability.

CHAPTER B4

TENDERING

Assuming the marketing and sales functions have been effective, a customer will invite the particular supplier to tender by means of an invitation to tender which will require an answer by a particular date. This answer, the tender, will take the form of a technical proposal, plus the price of the tender suitably broken down. Where the marketing and sales functions have really been effective the supplier will be the only company requested to tender—single action tender. Should this be the case, there is a temptation for the supplier to put less effort into the tender than would be the case if it were a competitive tender. This is an acceptable approach, but it must not be overdone because:

1. It could make the tender so weak the customer goes elsewhere.
2. Sufficient effort must be put into the tender to ensure that the prices, to be quoted to the customer, are accurate within the scope of normal commercial risk.

Whether the tender is single action or competitive the supplier must put together a team to produce the tender, along the lines shown in the Personnel Requirements section at the end of this chapter.

Apart from the issues of price and/or significant technical innovation, the customer may, even in a competitive situation, have a favoured supplier prior to formal tendering. The objective of the tender from this supplier, will be, therefore, to support and if possible strengthen the image created by marketing and sales. This assumes that the customer's perception of the image is the good one the supplier intended, otherwise drastic action is called for. Also it will provide ammunition for the supplier's supporters within the customer's organization to argue the supplier's case. Section A of this book advises customers not to let this happen; however, it is inevitable to some degree.

Where the customer is successful in this or the supplier himself does not know if one of the tendering suppliers is favoured, he should still use the proposal to support and if possible strengthen the image created by his marketing and sales function. This will include emphasizing his strong points and minimizing his weak points relative to the strengths and weaknesses of the competition, if this is known.

81

Where the supplier knows one of his rivals is favoured, the marketing and sales image again should be supported and the emphasizing of strong points and the minimizing of weak points should be made more in relation to this favoured competitor. This should not be done, however, to the exclusion of all thoughts of the other competitors.

Whether the supplier is favoured, not favoured, or simply does not know, he should cover all points raised in the invitation to tender and adhere to the tender procedures, particularly if they include a format for the tender. If the supplier perceives omissions in the invitation to tender, particularly on points which are favourable to him, he should insert these in such a way that he does not appear to be criticizing the customer for their omission. The most common of these is the supplier's corporate viability and hence his ability and 'desire' to provide support and expand the system, if required, throughout its life.

Assuming there are no significant flaws in a supplier's technical submission, the key parameter in who gets the contract will normally be price. Here the supplier must seriously consider his commercial risk if the customer requires a fixed price. His decision on whether to comply or suggest an alternative pricing arrangement, fixed price design followed by budgetary implementation, cost plus, etc. (see Chapter A2) is determined by balancing two considerations, namely:

1. The nearer to fixed price he goes the greater the commercial risk.
2. The further he departs from the customer's fixed price requirement, the greater his uncompetitiveness, particularly if his rivals go along with the customer's requirements.

The supplier's cost in implementing the customer's requirement will be largely determined by the amount of special-to-project software that requires writing. In addition to the direct cost of the amount, the performance requirements of the software design will influence the hardware requirements and hence the cost.

The estimation of the volume of software to be written can be estimated in a number of ways:

1. By a crude comparison with similar projects that the organization has completed (including any prototypes, simulations, or models of the projects).
2. By breaking the software down into its detailed modules and making the easier, more accurate estimation of module size and then accumulating them.
3. Using a software cost estimation model.
4. Validating the above estimates using a methodology based on the number of function points.

Answers from the three or more methods should be compared and the worst taken plus any elements of one of the totals that were not included in the worst estimate.

In turning this into a price, the cost of contingency sick and annual leave, unsocial hours working, etc. must be taken into account.

It is important to note that the base parameters in the above will be different for different organizations and even individuals within organizations. Customers will know that these differences can have a greater effect than other considerations like the language used, or the method of coding (batch or interactive) although these too should be considered. However, all the above means that all organizations should keep statistics on both their actual performance and their variation from estimated performance.

Consideration should be given to the use of standard packages, or existing software. Normally this will provide a means of keeping the overall price down. However, care should be exercised that any modification costs or performance penalties do not offset or more than offset this advantage.

All hardware and software sizing and hence costing should include some degree of contingency. The overall contingency should be estimated by an appropriate theory of errors. This will take into account all conceivable errors and the estimated probability that they might arise and will include a margin for unforeseen risks. The contingency figure arrived at should then be added to the overall cost of the project. Additional to the labour and equipment costs of the project the support costs should be added. These will include such items as computer time, computer maintenance during development, insurance, equipment room and office space, lighting, heating and power, etc. Some of these will not apply if development is being done on a computer that is later being delivered to the customer as part of the project. A check should also be made that these support elements will be available. This is particularly necessary for computer time if a general software development facility is going to be used. The manager of this facility should be consulted at all stages and kept informed of the progress of the tender so that he can update his own advance planning and so accommodate the project.

The sum of the labour, equipment and support costs will be the estimated total cost of the project if it is to be implemented within the customer's own computer organization. Should this computer organization be in direct competition with outside suppliers this cost should not be the only criterion that determines who gets the project. The ability of the internal department to do the job in terms of its expertise and to meet the timescale, taking into consideration its other commitments, should also be taken into account.

With a supplier, his marketing and sales function should indicate the likely winning price. This should be compared with the production cost price and a commercial decision taken on the price to be quoted to the customer. This will be accompanied by the supplier's suggestions for a stage payment plan. This may be in the form of comments on the customer's suggestion in the invitation to tender. It is assumed that the supplier does his detailed cash flow sums before doing this. Even if the quoted price is lower than the production cost, the supplier's project manager should still be given a budget equal to the estimated production cost. Sometimes he may be given a budget less than the production cost and charged with recouping the shortfall by an increased mark-up on change orders, extra equipment, spares, etc. that the customer might request. Alternatively the shortfall may be covered by an internal budget, probably from venture capital, on the understanding that the outcome is a standard product rather than just the individual customer's requirement.

PERSONNEL REQUIREMENTS

Ideally the tender should be produced by a team comprising those given below with the qualities listed.

USER

1. Extensive applications knowledge.
2. Significant computer knowledge.

COMPUTER

1. Extensive system design/analysis knowledge and experience.
2. Significant applications knowledge.
3. Significant engineering knowledge.
4. Extensive performance estimation and sizing knowledge and experience.

ENGINEERING

1. General engineering knowledge.
2. Significant computer knowledge.
3. Extensive knowledge and experience of the computer and communciations equipment market.

MARKETING/SALES

1. General sales/marketing.
2. Significant applications knowledge.
3. Necessary legal knowledge (see Section D).
4. Some computer knowledge.
5. Some engineering knowledge.

LEGAL

1. Extensive contract law.
2. Some computer knowledge.

ACCOUNTANT

1. Extensive Company financial knowledge.
2. Necessary legal knowledge (see Section E).
3. Some computer knowledge.
4. Some engineering knowledge.

The leader of the team will be drawn from user, computer, marketing and sales and will be the most experienced manager. Approval of the tender, particularly if there is a price reduction, will be undertaken by a senior manager within the company using a formal procedure.

CHAPTER B5
PRE-CONTRACT NEGOTIATIONS

The supplier's objective during the pre-contract negotiations is to expedite the signature of the contract between himself and the customer. This should not be done at the expense of projected unacceptable loss in profitability, nor where a loss-leading situation is involved, at the cost of an unacceptable increase in the loss. Neither should the objective be so pursued that an unacceptable increase in the commercial risk to the supplier is incurred.

The pre-contract negotiations will be conducted on behalf of the supplier by an appropriate senior manager supported by the team who produced the tender plus projected members of the design team.

This objective and its caveats are compatible with the customer's requirement to sort out ambiguities and omissions before the contract is signed. These ambiguities and omissions may be contractual or financial as well as technical. The supplier should be cautious in the way he draws attention to these ambiguities and omissions, particularly in the operational requirement, as the customer's staff responsible, who may have worked upon it for some years, might be sensitive to having their 'errors' pointed out.

For similar reasons an unsophisticated customer may not see the necessity for a joint functional specification which would overcome these ambiguities and omissions. The desirability of one should have been suggested to the customer prior to contract. If, however, the customer is adamant about there being no necessity for a joint functional specification, to replace his operational requirement, or at least changes to it, the supplier is faced with a difficult situation. Assuming the supplier has not included a cost for a joint functional specification in his price (and given a competitive pricing situation this is very probable) and he still wants the contract, he has no recourse but to let contract signature occur. He should then progressively point out the ambiguities and omissions to the customer during the early life of the contract, and insist that the customer raises change notes to correct them. These should then be costed in such a way as to cover all the costs incurred, not only the cost of implementing them, but also the cost incurred in discovering them. This is unsatisfactory but inevitable, because although the supplier has justified reasons for the inevitable project slippage, the odium will still count against him. The odium would of course be justified if the supplier had taken the operational requirement at its face value, not realizing the extent of the errors and omissions.

To reduce the commercial risks of the project the supplier will, at tender time (see Chapter B4), have decided the extent to which he can quote a fixed price in the tender commensurate with him getting the contract. Unless he feels he is carrying insignificant risk, he should be aware of any circumstances in the pre-contract negotiations that could lead him to re-opening the firm price quotation with the customer. This should be delicately handled to prevent the customer feeling that the supplier is reneging on his tender. However, if for instance a joint functional specification stage is introduced at this point; or the customer comes up with an immediate batch of change orders, these may present the supplier with the opportunity. He could then suggest that he can only confirm his amended fixed price after a joint Functional Specification is drawn up or the design stage is complete. Again he would reassure the customer if a limit of liability was agreed. Even if scope is left for the variation of the overall price after contract, the stage payments plan will be agreed during pre—contract negotiations. This is subject to each stage payment being expressed as a percentage of the overall price. The supplier can try to have a plan agreed that gives him a cost of money in his favour. In the unlikely event of this being agreed he can use the extra cash to increase his profit or reduce his price. Because he has, at this stage, all but won the contract he is unlikely to do this. However, it could be used as a reserve to offset the risks of a fixed price contract irrespective of the stage at which the implementation price becomes fixed.

PERSONNEL REQUIREMENTS

As already stated, the pre-contract negotiations will be conducted on behalf of the supplier by an appropriate senior manager supported by the team who produced the tender plus projected members of the design team.

CHAPTER B6
FUNCTIONAL SPECIFICATION

After contract signature the first major milestone will be the completion of the joint functional specification. The objectives and contents of this document are more fully described in Chapters A9 and D7.

The functional specification will also have the specific objective of being the basis of the supplier's detailed designers' and programmers' work and the work of his test team in preparing tests, particularly acceptance tests.

The functional specification will be produced by the supplier's design team (see Personnel Requirements, Chapter B7) with assistance and agreement on content from the customer's supplier monitoring team (see Personnel Requirements, Chapter A10).

The supplier's project manager will delegate the writing of different chapters to members of his team. They will have the facility of asking questions of nominated (by the customer) members of the customer's team. When they have completed their sections, they should be approved by the nominated persons in the customer's team. Finally, all the sections should be cross-checked and edited into a complete document. A senior member of the supplier's team should be made responsible for this—possibly the project manager himself. This document will be validated and submitted for final approval to the customer's project manager.

The supplier's project manager, in order to preserve project timescales, should insist that questions and requests for approval are responded to in a reasonable timescale (two days and two weeks respectively). Unless this is forthcoming he also should insist on his freedom to make assumptions, and to assume approval.

Once complete, the functional specification will be under the control of configuration management.

PERSONNEL REQUIREMENTS

The functional specification will be produced by the supplier's design team (see Personnel Requirements, Chapter B7).

CHAPTER B7

SYSTEM DESIGN (INCLUDING MODELLING)

The objective of the system design stage is a design which allows equipment to be procured and detailed software design and programming to commence, commonly termed implementation. The design will be undertaken by the design team with the skills shown in the Personnel Requirements section of this chapter.

Ideally the functional specification should be in existence before more detailed system design commences, but in practice system design will have commenced at the tender stage. Therefore the first task of system design after agreeing the joint functional specification, is to review the design work done at the tender stage and subsequently, with a view to its suitability for the revised requirement. Effectively system design will proceed in parallel with the production of the functional specification, since top-down design can proceed before detailed functions of the low-level units have been determined.

System design will commence by deciding upon the software structure, including standard items (particularly operating system characteristics) needed to meet the operational requirement. It should be specified using a program design methodology. A performance analysis should be done on this structure and, with the operational requirement and the users' preferences in mind, an appropriate choice of hardware made. (It is noted that not infrequently the customer will have made the hardware choice, in which case the above process must be somewhat amended.) This process is called software engineering and implies that normal engineering design principles are followed. The process should include the establishment of a comprehensive list of support software requirements and their top-level and interface design.

The performance analysis required above and that performed at the end of the design stage to give confidence that the design will meet the predicted loading requirements are best achieved by modelling the proposed design. Models can be simple paper calculations or a sophisticated presentation of proposed design characteristics in one of the several modelling languages that are available.

90

Whatever approach is adopted it is important that the assumptions under-lying the model and its input data are clearly understood. As the design and the design implementation proceeds these assumptions will change to a greater or lesser degree. It is absolutely vital that if the assumptions are changed the model is rerun with the modified assumptions, and if the design no longer meets the required performance the appropriate action is taken.

These assumptions can be changed by change notes. It is important that these change notes are applied to the functional specification under the control of configuration management (see Chapter C1). Specifically the effect of change notes on the performance model should be considered.

Once a hardware and software configuration has been chosen to meet the requirements of the system functioning normally under maximum load, further requirements should then be considered. These requirements include the availability, reliability (including recovery) and maintainability of the system. The latter should include the design of any support software items missing from the standard support software portfolio running on a hardware configuration suitable for software development and testing. Similar con-sideration should be given to the training requirements of both users and support personnel.

Finally the performance analysis should be repeated for the firmed-up hardware and software configuration. The predicted ability of the system to work under maximum loadings is paramount. The parameters that should be satisfied include response times, storage capacities, software and data volumes, communications channel speeds, etc. It should be noted at the time of writing this book computer performance analysis is a very inexact science. Normal engineering contingency margins are not enough. Safety factors should therefore be of the order of five to ten not two. Wherever possible computer processors should be chosen from ranges that permit the sub-stitution of faster processors than the ones estimated to be required, without software changes.

During the design process a series of design reviews should be held with persons present, external to the design team, playing devil's advocate. The design should be validated by an independent body, possibly the test or quality assurance team. Validation will consist of the verification of the design to show that it meets the designer's objectives and checking to see that the design meets all of the requirements in the functional specification.

Once an adequate design has been completed this should be frozen under configuration management and documented in the design specification (see Chapter D8) which will be only changed under configuration management.

PERSONNEL REQUIREMENTS

The design team should include one or more of the following personnel with the qualities listed.

COMPUTER

1. General system design experience.
2. Significant application knowledge.
3. Computer performance estimating ability.
4. Knowledge of the design methodology to be used.

USER

1. General applications knowledge.
2. Significant computer knowledge.

ENGINEER

1. General engineering knowledge.
2. Significant computer and communications knowledge.

The team leader will usually be the senior computer man, provided he has the necessary management skills.
To assess changes the following may be required:

LEGAL

1. General knowledge of corporate law.
2. Company knowledge.

ACCOUNTANT

1. General commercial knowledge.
2. Significant project knowledge.
3. Company knowledge.

CHAPTER B8

SYSTEM IMPLEMENTATION

The objective of system implementation is to produce a fully developed functioning and integrated system, in accordance with the functional specification, ready for acceptance testing. Ideally system implementation can only commence when the design stage is complete. However, where timescales are tight, the application is not complex nor performance critical and where top-down programming techniques have been used, the programming of the special-to-project software can commence once the functional specification is agreed. If this does occur it is essential that any code produced before agreement on the system design is checked to see that it conforms to the system design. Where it does not, it should be rewritten so that it does conform.

Where there is a contractually separate system design stage, obviously no programming can commence until the system design is agreed. Whatever the situation on system design, systems implementation will take place in parallel with testing (see Chapter B10) and documentation (see Chapter B14).

Systems implementation will be undertaken by the supplier's implementation team which will comprise individuals with the skills described in the Personnel Requirements section at the end of this chapter.

Where the supplier is a manufacturer, most or all of the hardware and standard software will be obtained by an intra-organizational transfer rather than by procurement. The introduction of this hardware and standard software to the implementation process will be phased in accordance with the demands of the process. Some of the procurements may pre-date the process requirements for purposes of buying and/or financial advantage, although the cost of storage and the possible effective loss of warranty time must also be considered.

The implementation will normally consist of the writing of special-to-project (usually applications) software and its integration with standard hardware and software. Some projects may require no special-to-project software. Hence these projects will proceed with all hardware and software being assembled and integrated into the full system, with testing taking place when appropriate.

The special-to-project software will be written by small teams. The number of teams will depend on the amount of software to be written. They may be

92

organized along chief programmer team lines and as an extension of this idea, the author has found it useful to include a user in each team to interpret requirements, suggest realistic module test data, etc. The software the teams are responsible for producing should fall into elements that follow the logical breakdown of the design.

The special-to-project software should be written top-down using a structured programming methodology.

The programming should nearly always be done in a high-level language. The reasons for this are the increases in programmer productivity, portability and maintainability that high-level languages offer over low-level ones. These should only be considered where the efficiency and performance of the software is hypercritical.

The writing of the software in a so-called 'fourth generation' or applications generator' language should be considered. This has particular attractions for speedy coding and programmer productivity, particularly in commercial data processing. If the applications generator is particularly close to the design methodology used it may reduce the programming effort considerably. It is highly appropriate for the development of prototype systems. Offsetting the advantages are the greater software inefficiency, lack of portability, and the problems that stem from these languages not always being universally available.

It is recommended that 'walk-throughs' be held at stages in the design and writing of programs. A walk-through is a structured meeting of a group of people to review a phase of the programmer's work, and to detect errors. The walk-through may take place at any or all of the following phases:

1. Program design.
2. Coding.
3. Test plan.
4. Writing of any relevent documentation.

Walk-throughs should be attended by:

1. The programmer's team.
2. Some programmers working in associated teams.
3. Some members of the quality assurance group.
4. Customer's representatives (optional).

No managers should attend. At least 48 hours before the walk-through, the material to be reviewed should be sent to all the participants which they should study. A chairperson should be appointed. His/her job will be to structure the meeting and to prevent it from digressing from its task of discovering errors. A secretary should also be appointed. His/her job is to prepare an action list of the errors and problems detected. Trivial errors such as syntax errors, inconsistent names, etc. , should not be recorded on the action list, but merely noted by the programmer. The chairperson and secretary should preferably be members of the quality assurance group described in Chapter B13, although this is not essential. The programmer must not be either chairperson or secretary. The action list should be duplicated to all participants immediately after the meeting. Within 2 working days, the programmer should note the action list with his resolution of the problems raised. This resolution need not necessarily involve change, for example further investigation might show that the supposed error was wrongly conceived. Quality assurance should examine the responses to certify that the actions taken are satisfactory.

The teams should test their own modules independently. When this testing of the module on its own is complete, it should be signed off by the chief programmer as being ready for submission to the test team. These tests should be planned and the results documented.

At a certain stage in the programming process, sufficient top-level modules will have been signed off for the test team to integrate them with standard hardware and software into the first test version of the system. This will then be tested and the resulting errors discovered referred back by discrepancy reporting (see Chapter C2) to the appropriate programming teams. They will then create modifications to these modules to correct the bugs, which after signing-off will be sent to the test team for integration into a subsequent test version of the system. At that time the test team will check the correction works. If not the discrepancy report stays open. In parallel with correcting these bugs the programmer team will be producing lower-order modules which will also go forward for incorporation into subsequent test versions of the system.

A cycle of building, testing, correcting and building again later and later test versions of the systems will be established until all the software is written and debugged (see Figure B8.1). The system is then ready for acceptance testing. As stated later in this chapter, it is highly desirable that the number of changes are kept to a minimum, however, some may be inevitable. A new version of the test system may therefore contain completely new modules and modified modules by reasons of corrections and changes. The process has to be carefully controlled so that a new version of the test system is not so completely new that it proves impossible to test. Conversely it is pointless, except at the very end of testing, to plan tests which probability indicates will not produce a worthwhile crop of errors. Given the situation where both new modules changes and corrections are being integrated into the same test system build, corrections should be given sufficient priority so that changes are applied against a reasonably stable base.

As soon as the first test system is set up, the partially complete system should be subject to source control under configuration management. Thenceforth, the programmers will lose control of their programs, and no changes may be made except under the authorized discrepancy reporting procedure (see Chapter C2) or change request procedure (see Chapter C1). Only the system build team will have access to the system to insert new or revised code. This will prevent programmers from the time-wasting pursuit

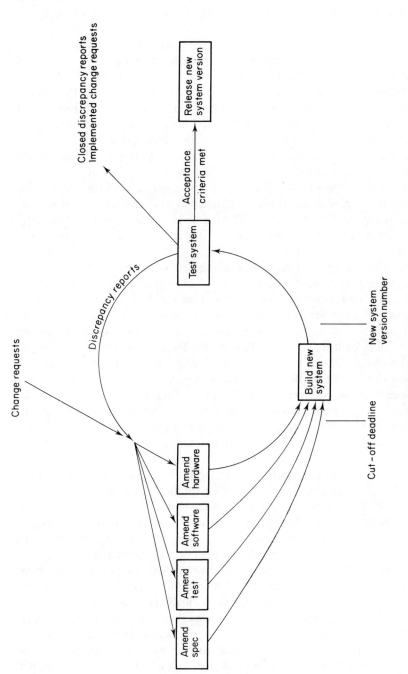

Figure B8   Build—Test—Correct Cycle.

of 'improving' modules which already perform their proper function, and will provide as stable a system as possible for lower-level modules to be added.

During the final phases of the build–test–correct–build cycle when all modules have been written, the system will become increasingly stable and implementation will primarily concern systems programmers, the system build section, test team, and engineers. The programming teams themselves will become under-occupied and so can be reduced in numbers. Because of the team concept those remaining will have sufficient knowledge of the code to fix the small number of bugs that are being discovered.

The system build section will keep records of which modules and which version of each module are contained in each test version of the system. They will keep records of the discrepancies discovered, with the test version they were discovered in and the test version they were corrected in. Similarly, changes, if any, will be chronicled. These data is not only needed for control of the current project but are vital for the cost and timescale of future projects.

Along with the production of operational software the support software will be programmed and tested. It will be subject to the same source control and configuration management and via the project plan will be kept functionally in step with the applications software. Depending on its size, and the criticality of the application, control may be less formal, with each package being built by its own programming team. However, the testing of support software should be the responsibility of the test team.

During the implementation process it is highly desirable that the number of change requests are kept to a minimum. This not only applies to the changes that are actually implemented but those that are put up for evaluation. Even these are a significant distraction to the implementation team and are a major factor in project slippage. Design changes should only be contemplated, during implementation, if the original design will not work or the total system implementation effort required is reduced by an amount greater than the resources required in effecting the design change. Functional changes should not be contemplated by the supplier between agreement on the joint functional specification and system acceptance. It is the supplier's contractual responsibility to meet this specification and the customer's to ensure that the specification meets the operational requirement. Inevitably the customer will become aware that the contractual functional requirement is diverging from the real operational requirement, particularly where the project has a long timescale to completion. However, if he is a sophisticated customer, he will appreciate that getting something working and then applying changes is invariably a better way of proceeding than creating a continuous moving target. Where the customer is naïve enough to insist on continuous change the supplier may decide it is in his commercial interest to go along with the customer's desires. If he does he should at all times inform the customer of the inevitable increased timescale (never talk of delays) and price.

The change control procedures can handle this, but it may be necessary to reinforce this with correspondence at a senior level. Although it may be commercially sensible for the supplier to accept the changes, the demotivating effect on his staff of a project without end should be considered.

PERSONNEL REQUIREMENTS

Most of the design team skills (preferably the same personnel) plus those given below with the qualities listed.

USER

1. General applications knowledge.
2. Significant computer knowledge.

COMPUTER

(a) 1. General programming in chosen language.
    2. Some applications knowledge.
    3. Knowledge of the structured programming technique to be used.
(b) 1. Specific systems programming skills in language, operating system and hardware involved.
    2. Some applications knowledge.

ENGINEERING

1. General engineering knowledge of hardware involved.
2. Some knowledge of the standard software involved.
3. Some applications.

The latter stages of implementation will be conducted in parallel with testing, for which the personnel requirements are detailed in Chapter B10.

CHAPTER B9

INSTALLATION

At some stage during the course of the project, equipment will require installing, either at the supplier's premises (factory) or the customer's premises (site). Normally installation will be carried out by the supplier's personnel or the subcontractor's personnel (generally the manufacturer). These personnel will have the skills described in the Personnel Requirements section at the end of this chapter.

Certain items of equipment may have to be installed twice (factory and site). The determining factor is generally where the software development and testing for the project is to be undertaken. Criteria which govern this include:

1. Is a general software development facility available?
2. Where are the greatest number of staff, customer and supplier, to be based? The customer's view is of course paramount.
3. Availability of space with the necessary works services on customer's premises (site) or supplier's premises (factory).
4. Are there specific requirements for early installation of equipment on site?
5. What are the costs and risks of installation or reinstallation which may include extra transport, cabling, testing, and insurance, etc.
6. How many non-project pieces of equipment does the system have to be interfaced with?
7. Is the system a single one or can it be split up and useful work performed on the bits?
8. What are the overall costs of the different approaches?

All factors, particularly standards pertinent to installation, will be described in an installation requirements document (see Chapter D10). This document may be a customer's standard publication applicable to all installation work on his premises or it may be a document produced specially for the project. Whatever the case, to adhere to it should be contractually agreed between customer and supplier and as such it will have been referred to in the invitation to tender. Should one not exist, the supplier would be well advised to draw one up soon after contract signature and get the customer's agreement to it. Irrespective of the installation requirements document's origins all installation should be carried out in accordance with it. The document ideally should come under configuration management, but, his may be a problem if the document is more general than the area covered by configuration management.

The contract may or may not make the prime supplier responsible for the works services at the customer's site or sites. Indeed, the responsibility could be split, with different responsibilities for works services at the site of the main computer complex and works services at remote sites. In any case, whatever the responsibilities, works services at a particular location must be complete before installation can commence at that location. Works services can be summed up as building, lighting, environment (a particularly tight specification for most computers, down to dust content of the air), power supplies and cabling.

The supplier should have ensured, or been assured by the customer, that there will be no physical problems in moving the computer equipment in at the time installation is planned. If there are doubts on this score, he should check carefully the physical dimensions and floor-loading capacities of all points on the equipment access route. Particular items to be checked are doors, ramps and lifts. If bottlenecks are discovered thought will have to be given to unconventional access methods, e.g. via cranes through external windows.

Assuming all installation standards, works services and access factors have been considered, some general points still require covering:

1. Equipment should be tested after every move, sufficient to ensure it has not been damaged by the move.
2. Wherever software development and testing are taking place adequate provision must be made for the personnel involved, both in terms of office space and in access to the machine by way of physical proximity and attachment of development VDUs, etc. This should be covered contractually.
3. The supplier's installation engineer must have right of access before (site inspection), during and after (maintenance) installation. Along with this access go the working space, conditions and power supplies to enable him to do his job. This is particularly true if the possibility exists of simultaneous work occurring with customer's or other supplier's personnel. This should be covered contractually.

PERSONNEL REQUIREMENTS

Installation will be carried out by the personnel given below with the qualities listed below.

ENGINEERING

1. General installation engineering knowledge

2. Knowledge of the specifics of the particular computer and communications equipment being installed.

It is likely the professional engineer will be supported by appropriate technicians.

CHAPTER B10
TESTING

It is vital that all elements of the system are tested at all stages of integration and assembly from component and program modules. This will increase the probability that defects are detected as early as possible in the implementation process when their correction can be most easily accommodated rather than later in the process when the higher level of integration achieved makes their detection and solution much more difficult. Thus defects are less likely to cause delays and budget overruns.

All integration and system testing will be conducted by a test team which will comprise individuals with the skills described in the Personnel Requirements section at the end of this chapter. The team will be led by a manager reporting to the supplier's project manager. Some members of the test team may be customer's user personnel. These will be particularly useful in supplying the team with the necessary applications knowledge.

Soon after contract signature, both customer and supplier will agree on a test plan (see Chapter D9). This will contain a detailed chronology of all tests. The anticipated date of the tests will be shown, along with dates for the availability of the test scripts and their anticipated results.

The criteria for passing the tests will be shown with responsibilities for carrying them out. A descriptive list of test tools, both hardware and software, will be included, plus the procedures for setting up, performing, approving and chronicling the results of tests. The need for full or representative data files or databases will be noted, with criteria for their comprehensiveness and the responsibility for setting them up.

Testing will fall into four categories:

1. Functional
2. Performance
3. Structured. Here the logical structure of the software is tested and unlike the other tests a more detailed knowledge of the software design is required.
4. Extremes and anomalies. It is important that the system is seen to cope satisfactorily with extreme cases or anomalies. It should not simply fail, but give an output, possibly requesting manual intervention while processing other work, as far as possible, normally.

Testing of the system will commence as soon as implementation starts and will proceed in parallel with it until the system is ready for acceptance testing. Testing might even be considered to start before implementation if design reviews are considered to be part of the testing.

Hardware, firmware and standard software are assumed to be *not* special to project and therefore no special-to-project tests should be carried out on these except performance tests. The project management should be confident that the production tests that are carried out on these elements are normally satisfactory and are in fact applied to all supplied elements. (It is acknowledged that actual visual observation of all components will not always be possible and that assuring oneself that a test procedure exists and is executed will often have to suffice.)

Considering the sequence of the test process, it is important to realize that a *tested* subset of the final hardware, firmware and standard software complex must be available before software testing can commence. The special-to-project software of a system will be then tested top-down. All other testing should be conducted bottom-up. Final system testing will be conducted with all elements of the system hardware, software, firmware and operating personnel and procedures present. The general sequence of testing will normally follow the following pattern:

Test of representative hardware, firmware and standard software subset.

Test of all support software relevent to testing.

Test Applications Software up to complete applications software package.

Test of remaining support software.

Test of missing hardware, firmware and standard software items.

Test of applications package on complete hardware, firmware and standard software complex.

Test of applications package on complete complex with operational personnel running and using the system.

Plan and test scripts could be treated as two separate documents. The test plan lays down what testing must be done, and should be produced early in the project and put under configuration management control. Preparation of test scripts is a time-consuming task and may even not be possible before a test is ready. To await completion of the test scripts before putting the test plan under configuration management would be advisable.

The following points should guide the execution of the test plan:

1. Test scripts and anticipated results will be subject to configuration management and hence change controls and changes should be checked by regression testing. (The results, from revised test script applied to revised software, should be compared with the original test results and the difference checked against the anticipated results of the change.)
2. All elements of the test, script, software anticipated results, test aids, etc. should have a modification or version number. It should not be

assumed that the results of a test conducted with one set of modification or version numbers will be the same as a test conducted with a different set. If there is the slightest doubt the test should be repeated with the new sequence.

3. The test scripts should in general be composed of data that are as near to real life as is possible. However, a part of the testing should include bizarre test data to check that the system can cope generally, through its error routines.

4. Where applicable, a test database, which will be used for all high-level testing, must be prepared before script writing commences. It should then be subject to source control (see Chapter B8), so that alterations which would invalidate test results can be avoided. In general, changes would normally be allowed but only after careful scrutiny.

5. Test tools could include a package for constructing test scripts with the ability to merge scripts for higher assembly level testing; a package to construct anticipated results and compare them with actual results, or other recorded test results (for regression testing), and annotate the differences (see Chapter B15).

6. The criteria for passing a test should be expressed in terms of the Discrepancy Reporting system (see Chapter C2). The test will not be considered successful if any priority 1 discrepancies are discovered (discrepancies which make the system operationally unacceptable) or if above a specified number of each of the other priorities are found to be present.

7. It is not considered sensible for the test team to conduct the lowest level of testing. This should be the responsibility of the production section responsible for the item. Software modules that are the responsibility of individual programmer teams will be tested in isolation by that team. It is the responsibility of the chief programmer responsible for that module to say that it is ready for handing over to the test team. He will assess this by consideration of the programmers' own testing results, through his structured walk-through, etc. Problems caused by premature or delayed handover will be dealt with between the chief programmer and the test manager with the intervention of higher management (project manager) where appropriate.

Individual tests should be carried out in the following manner. If the test is passed then a test report should be filed and testing can then be continued. If at any stage in the later production process the modification or version status of the system element is changed from that used in the test, *serious* consideration should be given to repeating the test and all dependent higher-level tests. The test should certainly be repeated if a different version of the item under test is to be used in the operational system. A test report is also filed if the test is unsuccessful, then the element under test is referred back to the appropriate production authority. In the majority of cases this will be one of the software teams. The person(s) conducting the test will always try to bypass discrepancies that stop the test running to completion, after observing and recording all facts relevant to the discrepancy. The usefulness of the test will thus be maximized. Generally it will not be advantageous to conduct a test in the next level of the test hierarchy if a constituent element has failed its test at the lower level.

Performance tests present particular problems especially when the maximum load on the system is to be tested. It will not always be possible or cost effective to create this load manually. Techniques such as a simulation package must be used to create the maximum load in a controlled manner using as realistic as possible permutations of live data. The monitoring of performance tests will involve the use of such tools as hardware and software monitors and response time monitoring may involve the actual observation of VDU responses using stop-watches.

Wherever possible all tests should be conducted using the regression principle. This means that if a test is repeated with an alteration to the test or the system, the change is assumed not to have caused errors in the unchanged portions of the test or system. Therefore, test results from these areas, which are identical, need only be checked to see if they are identical and not analysed further. Also, the differences in the results of the test need only be examined to see if they correspond to the anticipated change in results. This saves significant time, particularly if the process is automated using the computer itself and a special support software package.

All tests, whether successful or unsuccessful, should be documented with a test report with the contents described in Chapter D9.

It can be seen that in many ways the test team is central to the production process and it may be appropriate for the test team to be responsible for the system build process also.

PERSONNEL REQUIREMENTS

System testing will be carried out by the personnel given below with the qualities listed.

USERS

1. Detailed knowledge and understanding of the Functional Specification.
2. Some computer knowledge, particularly of test tools.
3. Attentive to detail.

COMPUTER

1. General computer knowledge.
2. Particular systems knowledge, specifically performance analysis and support tools.

3. System testing experience.
4. Attentive to detail.

ENGINEER

1. Some applications knowledge.
2. General engineering knowledge.
3. Ability to use hardware diagnostic tools.
4. General computer and communications knowledge.
5. General applications knowledge.
6. Attentive to detail.

System building will be carried out by personnel with the qualities listed below.

1. Some applications knowledge.
2. Some computer knowledge.
3. General project knowledge.
4. Ability to use system build tools.
5. Clerical ability.

CHAPTER B11

TRAINING

The introduction of a new computer system will require personnel both to use and support the system. It is highly probable that the skills that these personnel require will not be found in the customer's organization. The customer therefore has the option of training his own staff or recruiting. Normally he will opt for training his user staff because they are already familiar with the company and the particular application. Training existing staff also avoids the possible problems and expense of making staff redundant. Support staff (programmers, etc.) are more likely to be recruited, nevertheless the shortages of these may make the supplier also opt for training existing staff for support roles. It is therefore highly probable that before the system can go operational a large number of the customer's staff will require training.

It is normal in the turnkey situation for this training to be provided by the supplier. For this he will utilize personnel possessing the skills described in the Personnel Requirements section at the end of this chapter. As mentioned above, the training requirements for any large system fall into two categories. The first is the training of the users of the system, the second the support personnel.

USER TRAINING

There will be a unique course for the actual day-to-day users of the system. This course will be unique in that it will only apply to this system. It may, however, contain elements of manufacturer's standard courses where appropriate. Depending on the number of users to be initially trained and the ongoing user training requirements, user training may be accomplished by the supplier first training a number of the customer's personnel who then act as instructors to the remainder of the customer's users. The presence of a training function within the customer's organization will influence the approach adopted.

The timing of training is critical, and obviously it must be done before the system is used operationally. However, training people long in advance of them using their newly acquired skills is not only wasteful in terms of the inevitable forgetting that must occur but also has the negative effect of frustrating the trainee who wants to practise his/her new skills immediately.

It is possible that a small group will be required to be trained in advance of the main body of users. They will be required in such areas as system testing, etc. If the approach adopted is that of customer trainers the courses of this first group and the intended trainers could well be synchronized.

All training where possible should have a practical as well as a theoretical base. This will also dictate when the courses can be held, due to availability of equipment, etc.

A course for user (and other, if appropriate) management may also be required. While this should give the manager an appreciation of what his staff is required to do, it should concentrate on the general principles of the system rather than specific details. One area where it will be more specific is the procedures for system failure, particularly if judgements have to be made to revert to other methods (e.g. manual) of providing the function.

SUPPORT STAFF TRAINING

The computer support staff (programmers, operators, etc.) training will be a variable mixture of manufacturer's standard courses and special-to-project courses. The practice of manufacturers to include in their equipment price the cost of a certain number of attendances of their courses should be noted. The manufacturers generally list the prerequisite knowledge required before attendance on a course and care should be taken to see individuals have this. Engineering support staff normally will have their training requirements met by standard courses.

As with users, the timing of the courses is of importance and manufacturers' courses can be held at infrequent intervals and be oversubscribed, thus requiring early booking. One answer, which is also cheaper, is to arrange the courses on the customer's premises. This is only possible, if the practical training requirement is to be met, where the customer has equipment installed and available. The purchase of a separate training configuration is dependent on similar criteria to that for a support and development facility, plus the question of whether the number of people to be trained justifies a dedicated training facility. Consideration should also be given to accommodating the training function on the support and development configuration. Where a training facility is justified, it is often required in advance of the main configuration. Early training can thus be carried out on less tested versions of the operational software. This should be taken into account in the preparation and planning. Manufacturers' course prerequisites were referred to earlier and these should also be considered for special-to-project courses, e.g. if an insufficient number of VDU operator users have the ability to use a keyboard, a special typing techniques course may well be required.

All those present on courses should be supplied with course notes and copies of other documentation (e.g. the functional specification) where appropriate. Where a significant amount of training is required a training specification document (see Chapter D11) should be produced by the supplier. This will contain details of all courses with their subject matter, applicability and prerequisites. All training documentation should be under configuration management (see Chapter C1) and a schedule of courses should be part of the project plan (see Chapter C3).

Some of the courses that could be provided include:

Introduction to programming;
Specific languages;
Applications programming;
System programming;
Support systems;
programming;
Job control language;
Operating system;
Hardware maintenance;
Operator training;
Database management;
User training;
User management training;
Support management training;
(NB. This list is not comprehensive.)

PERSONNEL REQUIREMENTS

The instructors, training users, will require:

1. Training skills.
2. Significant application knowledge.
3. Some computer and engineering knowledge.
4. Knowledge of the particular system.

The instructors, training computer personnel, will require:

1. Training skills.
2. Significant appropriate computer and engineering knowledge.
3. Knowledge of the particular system.

CHAPTER B12
ACCEPTANCE TESTING

The objectives in performing acceptance testing from the customer's stand-point are described in Chapter A11. Acceptance testing is also important from the supplier's standpoint in several ways:

1. The passing of acceptance tests is generally the condition which must be satisfied, before several stage payments are made. These include the final acceptance test which generally precedes the system going operational, and on which the large penultimate stage payment depends.
2. The acceptance tests, particularly the final one, give the supplier and the supplier's staff goals to aim at which are effective in concentrating the supplier's collective mind.
3. The final acceptance when complete represents the point when the supplier's main effort on the project is over with just warranty and maintenance effort remaining.

Acceptance testing will also cover the activities which in other disciplines are described as commissioning.

Acceptance testing will be carried out by the test team which comprise personnel possessing the skills described in the Personnel Requirements section of Chapter B10. The test team could of course include customer's personnel. Extra customer's personnel will be required to observe the accept-ance tests and some of these may be at a more senior level. The skills required for individuals performing the observer role will be similar but with less detailed knowledge of the specifics of testing. Their application and system knowledge must, however, be as high. All involved should be aware of the management procedures used during the testing process. A set of trained operational users will also be required.

The acceptance tests for the system should form an integral part of the main test plan (see Chapter D9) and as such should be specified and agreed with the customer (including criteria for passing), early in the life of the project.

Acceptance testing will normally take place at the system level. Acceptance tests will only take place below this level where individual elements of the system are required in advance of the main system, e.g. a computer configuration for user staff training.

Comprehensiveness should be the key feature of all acceptance testing with both functional and performance testing carrying equal weight. Particular attention should be paid to security (all types) and recovery features.

The acceptance tests should be carried out under conditions as near as possible to those found in operational use. These should include operational customer personnel using the system procedures. The data used should be live operational data wherever practicable. It should not be the data used in normal testing, except perhaps for the main database where the effort to create two databases for testing would be wasteful. The database referred to in Chapter B10 should therefore be used on the basis that every effort possible has been taken to make it realistic.

The criteria for passing the tests should be expressed in terms of discrepancy reports (Chapter C2). These criteria will obviously not let a test be passed if any discrepancies exist which make the system unsuitable (unsafe) for operation use. The test may, however, be passed if discrepancies exist which are undesirable or which are inconvenient. The number of discrepancies of each type which may be tolerated before the test is declared a failure should form the criteria for acceptance, agreed at an early stage in the test plan. The criteria should specify a time limit within which the discrepancies are fixed. Until then the test is passed conditionally.

Errors caused by users, procedures or data should form the basis of discrepancy reports as well as system errors. However, a method will be agreed as part of the test plan to arbitrate on whether a particular discrepancy report from a non-system error should be included in the criteria for passing the test.

All acceptance tests, upon successful completion, should have a formal sign- off by the appropriate customer manager designated in the test plan.

PERSONNEL REQUIREMENTS

Acceptance testing will be carried out by the test team which will include personnel possessing the job skills referred to in the Personnel Requirements section of Chapter B10. They will be observed by the customer's personnel (probably the supplier monitoring team) possessing the job skills specified in Personnel Requirements section of Chapter A10. Trained general system users will also be required. They will be the personnel who will be the actual operational users of the system.

CHAPTER B13

QUALITY ASSURANCE

The main objective of quality assurance in a computer project is to ensure the production of a quality maintainable product on schedule, within budget, and in compliance with the functional and performance requirements. Quality assurance is thus the responsibility of everyone involved with the project. However, the assurance is achieved by the supplier having a separate and specialist quality assurance group to lay down the standards and perform random checks that they are being observed. Everyone else will perform quality control by seeing that the standards are adhered to everywhere. This group will be staffed by personnel possessing the skills described in the Personnel Requirements section at the end of this chapter. The group will be managed by a supplier's executive, who will not report to the project manager. Preferably he will not even report to the same supplier's management as the project manager but to a specialist quality assurance and auditing function.

For every project a quality assurance plan for the project will be produced as soon after contract signature as possible, even before the jointly agreed functional specification. This plan will document directly or by reference all requirements standards reviews, audits and responsibilities which are required to ensure that the project is on schedule, within budget, in compliance with the functional and performance requirements, and of the necessary quality. Chapter D12 lists the contents of the quality assurance plan. The reason why the quality assurance manager does not report to the project manager is to ensure that no expedients are introduced to obtain any one goal at the expense of other project goals.

Normally quality assurance will concentrate on the special-to-project element on the basis that all other items are standard products. It is in these 'special-to-project' elements that quality assurance objectives are less likely to be met. The project quality assurance team will check, however, that there is an adequate quality assurance function (it need not be known by this name) involved in the production of standard products.

The quality assurance team will function, not only by participation in walk-throughs, design reviews as described elsewhere, but also by both regular and spot checks that quality (i.e. sufficiently high standards) is being maintained in all facets of the project.

In so far as the 'special-to-project' element is concerned, quality assurance will be involved in the main areas of specification design, implementation (particularly programming) and testing.

PERSONNEL REQUIREMENTS

The quality assurance team will be staffed principally with experienced computer and computer management personnel plus a small experienced engineer and engineering management function. This will be larger if special-to-project hardware is involved. A user element will be present to ensure the functional quality of the system.

CHAPTER B14

DOCUMENTATION

The amount and complexity of the information about a computer system is so vast that it is beyond the capacity of one person to memorize it, even if that person had perfect recall. Spreading the memorizing over several individuals may not necessarily solve the problems and new problems of communciation and subjectivity are introduced. Also it is highly unlikely that all the individuals with the knowledge will be available throughout the life of the system. All aspects of the system, must therefore, be documented.

The documentation will be produced by the person most intimately connected with the element of the project being documented and who possesses the skills specified in the Personnel Requirements section at the end of this chapter.

A technical editor will be needed on large projects. He will edit the contributions written by the various other members of the team and assemble them to form the requisite documents. He will ensure that the appropriate standards are adhered to. He will be responsible for controlling the documents under configuration management. Versions of each document will all be carefully numbered so that everybody concerned can ensure that they have the latest version. A word-processing capability, which could be provided by the support and development facility (Chapter B15) is an essential tool for any but the smallest documentation task.

There are a multiplicity of documentation standards available. An invitation to tender will normally specify one. However, the supplier should gently persuade the customer that the supplier's own standard meets his requirement (assuming it does) and that documenting in an alien standard will only mean unnecessary extra expense.

Whatever the standard, the documentation will divide itself up into several categories as shown below. It is important that a means exists for cross-referencing between associated elements of the different categories, not only so that a means exists for accessing information and so that the documents can be kept in step as they are updated, but also to ensure that the needs of configuration control are fulfilled.

Chapter D20 of this book gives a checklist for all the system documents.

We shall now consider the various categories of documentation that are required to define the system once it is complete. The purely project documentation is described in the appropriate chapters.

FUNCTIONAL

The document that describes what functions the system performs is the supplier/customer agreed functional specification. This document is more fully described in Chapters A9, B6 and D7.

DESIGN

There is a need for a document which describes the design of the system. This is the design specification, the contents of which are listed in Chapter D8.

This document tells how the design meets the functional requirements of the system. The document lists all the major elements, hardware and software, of the design and describes how they integrate together with the user and support procedures. The document references the hardware and software documents which describe individual elements of the design.

SOFTWARE

The software documentation should be structured so that it conforms with the structure of the software itself. For ease of maintenance it is suggested that the description of a software module is contained on a unique integral number of pages. The lowest level of documentation of the software is the source listings themselves which should include sufficient comment lines for this purpose. Above that there should be software design documents for each module and group of modules with an overall design document for each element of operational, support and diagnostic software. This will contain the top-level structure diagram for each of these elements of software along with conventions used, sizing information, etc.

The documentation that describes how the software is to be used differs for each of the three elements. The operational software usage is described in both the functional documentation and the user's procedures manuals referred to below. Support software will have a user manual for each program or package within the overall support software suite. The user manuals for diagnostic software are described under hardware below. All user manuals will give a comprehensive list of all output messages and their meaning, including error conditions. The contents of software documentation are covered in Chapter D18.

HARDWARE

At the lowest level the hardware will be described by wiring diagrams, although these will have less and less relevance in the age of VLSI circuits with fault correction being effected by the simple replacement of the defective card. Each hardware unit will have a document describing it, and there will be an overall document showing how the various units are linked together into the total system. This document will also show how the principal items of software link to the hardware units.

The use of each unit and indeed the whole system in normal operational use and when failures have to be coped with will be described in the procedures manuals. However, the hardware documentation will describe how to diagnose and correct the actual hardware faults if they are found to be the reason for the failure. The principal aid to diagnosis is diagnostic software and it is a moot point whether the user manuals for this software are separate or are contained in the appropriate hardware documentation. Once again the user manuals will give a comprehensive list of all output messages and their meaning, including error conditions. The contents of hardware documentation are covered in Chapter D17.

PROCEDURES

A procedural handbook will be written for each functional task undertaken by users and every task undertaken by support personnel. This will entail a certain amount of duplication. To overcome this, these handbooks could be structured, e.g. for an explanation of an error message a handbook might refer to a general manual of error messages. The author believes that, if at all possible, each user should have an individual handbook, which would entail extending configuration control to maintaining the currency of each handbook.

Both types of procedural handbook (operational and support) should not only cover procedures for operating the system but also the manual procedures that are connected with it, e.g. the methods for booking VDU connect time in a programming shop.

A procedures manual will also be required for the support and development facilities used by the project (see Chapter B15).

TESTING

Additional to the project test plan all tests should be documented so that they can be used as support and development aids during the life of the project. Their documentation should include their test scripts and anticipated results and the applicability of the tests, etc. The contents of a particular tests document are listed as part of Chapter D9.

TRAINING

Both operational and support personnel will require training. While such training, particularly during the later stages, will utilize the main system documentation, specific training documentation will be required in the following areas:

1. As lead-in material where the full system documentation will be too complex for introductory purposes.
2. To provide question and answer texts, for testing whether the learning is being acquired.
3. As a guide to the training itself, particularly if a simulator or emulator is used during the training process.

All the above documents for the project will be produced to a consistent standard. The standard will be specified at the outset of the project. The quality assurance manual will call for adherence to it and the quality assurance function will check that the standard is being adhered to; although primary responsibility lies with the first-line management of the respective teams.

PERSONNEL REQUIREMENTS

Functional documentation will be produced by the personnel given below with the qualities listed.

USERS

1. General application knowledge.
2. Significant computer knowledge.
3. Significant system knowledge.
4. Technical writing ability.

Software documentation will be produced by the personnel given below with the qualities listed.

COMPUTER

1. Particular system knowledge.
2. General computer knowledge.
3. Significant application knowledge.
4. Technical writing ability.

Engineering/equipment documentation will be produced by the personnel given below with the qualities listed.

ENGINEERING

1. Particular system knowledge.
2. General engineering knowledge.
3. Some computer and communications knowledge.
4. Some applications knowledge.
5. Technical writing ability.

TECHNICAL EDITOR

1. Qualified technical writer.
2. Detailed knowledge of documentation standards.

It should be noted that some documentation is a function of two or more disciplines, e.g. functional specification—user, computer and engineering.

SUPPORT AND DEVELOPMENT FACILITY

The implementation and testing of the special-to-project software and staff training will require a computer(s) from the same range as the operational configuration. Additionally a good deal of design work and management will be undertaken using software tools which will require a computer(s). The designated operational configuration may be available for this work but this may not always be so. Certainly if the system is to be developed after going operational (irrespective of policy this always seems to happen) and there is no spare capacity on the operational configuration a separate one will be required. Whatever configuration is utilized will, along with the support software tools, training software and the staff to operate and support them, comprise the support and developement facility.

The support and operations staff in this facility will require the skills described in the Personnel Requirements section at the end of this chapter.

We have considered two ways in which the computer configuration of the facility can be provided. The full set of possibilities for the implementation, testing and operational phases are as follows:

1. Use the designated operational computer configuration.
2. Use the suppliers general software support and development facility.
3. Use a third-party bureau facility. (NB. If remote VDU are provided staff need not be moved to this facility.)
4. Provide a configuration(s) dedicated to the support.
5. Provide combinations of the above.

Careful consideration should be given to check which is the most convenient and cost-effective way of proceeding subject to a sufficiency of computer time being provided at all times. What is sufficient in terms of configuration depends greatly on the requirements of the operational system. For an operational system which is live only for a limited time and has low integrity requirements, the necessary number of support and development terminals should happily be accommodated on the operational configuration to give an adequate support and development capability. The other extreme is a continuously operational high integrity and reliability operational system where it is vital that resilience must be tested and the operational configurations cannot be made available for this. Here the support and development configuration must be a near-copy of the operational system including multiple processors. The only difference is that most of the operational peripherals will not be required as the full load can easily be simulated. There will be a requirement for extra terminals for program development etc. Extra terminals should be provided so that there is always greater than one to every two project team members.

The support and development configuration must be able to function in two modes:

1. As a bureau running compilations of programs and test scripts, analysing test results, building new systems, etc.
2. As a replica of the operational system running full operational system, tests and training sessions.

It may be convenient to run each mode on a different configuration.

In all the above methods for providing a support and development facility it is important that all personnel with a need to use the facility, customer or supplier, will work flexible hours (e.g. will they regularly work nights to perform system tests, etc?).

Where the support and development facility is shared between several groups, the scheduling of the facility is necessary. This tactical scheduling is a function of 'data control' which normally will schedule the facility a week in advance. Means should be available to accommodate 'panic' situations and allow some flexibility in the schedule. Care should be taken to see that the system is not abused. Here internal accounting would help, with 'panic' computer time being at a premium. (NB. 'Data Control' is the administrative/clerical function which controls and monitors all work, to and from the facility.) Strategic scheduling of the facility should be one of the functions of the facility manager who will monitor the long-term (greater than six months) loading on the facility. He should be responsible for making timely proposals for additions and changes to the configuration and be authorized to use bureaux and second-hand purchases if so required.

The support and development facility will also require a data preparation capability. This can vary in size from one machine used by technical staff to a full data preparation department with specialist operators where a large volume of data has to be keyed-in, verified and checked before the system becomes operational.

We shall now consider the software tools that are required for the support and development facility:

1. *Bureau operating system.* It is possible that the operational operator system is a manufacturer's standard suitable also for bureau work. If not, a separate bureau operating system must be utilized with the disadvantages of maintaining two systems.

120

2. *Software production tools*. These will include compilers, assemblers debugger, test harness, core dump analysers, etc.
3. *System build tools*. These will be suits of programs taking the object code modules from the compilers and assembling them into operational packages; at the same time keeping track of all version numbers, unresolved linkages, etc.
4. *Fixed data assemblers*. To make the operational software flexible it will be written without any hard coded data so that changes in the operational environment or the computer configuration can be incorporated without a total rebuild of all the software. A package will be required to check this test data syntactically.
5. *Simulation data assembler*. A package will be required to check test scripts syntactically and assemble them into simulation data capable of being read in by the operational system in simulation mode.
6. *Test analyser*. The operational system will produce a log of its transactions. The amount of detail to be recorded can be a variable. A software package will be required to analyse the log. The same package should have the facility to compare two logs and list differences. This will significantly facilitate regression testing. Included in this package could be the analysis proportion of a software monitor, although in general a hardware monitor is to be preferred to avoid the disadvantage of a software monitor, namely that itself uses the computer.
7. *Project management tools*. It would be sensible if the project management tools used for the project such as programme evaluation and review technique (PERT), document control, etc. ran on the support and development configuration.
8. Word Processing — All documentation for the project should be produced on a word processor. In certain situations it might be convenient if the word processing took place on the support and development configuration.
9. *Diagnostic software*. Software will be required to perform fault diagnosis on both computer and communications hardware. Ideally this should run under the support operating system, although this may not always be possible if the operating system is not designed with this in mind. In that case the diagnostic software will run under its own operating system.

It is vital that all the above software tools are controlled under configuration management except the project management and word processing ones. However, it is probably prudent that no exceptions are made and even these are included.

All the procedures associated with running a support and development will be chronicled in a procedures manual. Among the procedures that this will describe are:

1. Operation of the computer.
2. Maintenance procedures, both planned and emergency.

3. Data control procedures (including media librarianship and data preparation).
4. Job submission procedures.
5. Scheduling procedures.
6. Procedures for user/facility communication and liaison.
7. Provision of consumables (e.g. magnetic tapes).

PERSONNEL REQUIREMENTS

The users of the support and development facility are classified under all other chapter headings such as Project Implementation, Testing, etc. and will not be repeated here.

Those responsible for the support and development of the software tools will be as given below with the qualities listed.

COMPUTER

1. General programming in chosen language.
2. Some applications knowledge.

If the amount of support and development software justifies it, the following would be a valuable asset to the support software team.

USER

1. General applications knowledge;
2. Significant computer knowledge.

Those responsible for the support and development configuration will fall into the following classes with the qualities listed.

MANAGEMENT

1. General management.
2. Significant computer knowledge, particularly operations.

OPERATION

1. Specific computer operating skills for bureau and operational system.
2. Knowledge of procedures.

ADMINISTRATION

1. Ability to operate chosen data preparation device and punch; key to disc, etc. (if required).

DATA CONTROL

1. General administrative/clerical ability.
2. Knowledge of system and organisation.
3. Knowledge of bureau procedures.

TAPE AND DISC LIBRARIAN

1. General library skills.
2. Knowledge of computer media.
3. Knowledge of bureau procedures.

DATA PREPARATION

1. Keyboard skills.

CHAPTER B16

WARRANTY AND MAINTENANCE

Most customers will request 12 months' warranty for all aspects of the system, sometimes with a request that support (maintenance and spares) is guaranteed for up to 10 years. The supplier should normally be pleased to meet this request.

Warranty and maintenance will fall into three categories:

1. Preventative hardware warranty or maintenance.
2. Hardware fault fixing warranty or maintenance.
3. Software fault fixing warranty or maintenance.

The supplier should insist that if he is to provide (2) he must also provide (1). Also, it would be more convenient if he provides (3) that he provides (1) and (2) also.

There are many possible variations for the arrangements between customers and suppliers for the provision of warranty and maintenance, particularly if development of the system is also to take place. Chapter A13 should also be carefully read to give a fuller picture of the possibilities.

The supplier has options in how he presents the price of warranty to the customer:

1. He can include the cost of all work in the warranty period in the total cost of the project.
2. He can include the cost of all work in the warranty period in the total cost of the project for preventative hardware maintenance for which he gives a separate quotation.
3. He can load the cost of all work in the warranty period on to the separately quoted cost for preventative hardware maintenance. He will then give different prices for the cost as the first year's maintenance and subsequent years' maintenance. Generally these will be lower, as the first year's maintenance will have to absorb the cost of fixing the early teething troubles, both software and hardware.

Option (3) and to a lesser extent option (2) have the advantage of the cosmetic exercise of making the capital cost of the project appear less. This approach has some justification because the supplier can be more confident

124

in taking responsibility for the trouble-free operation of the system if he has total control over it.

The normal means for providing the different categories of maintenance (which will now also mean warranty) are as follows. Preventative and fault fixing maintenance for manufacturers' standard hardware and software will be provided by manufacturers. The supplier, if he is responsible for these categories of maintenance, will thus subcontract this maintenance to the manufacturer under standard manufacturer's maintenance agreements. The only work the supplier himself will have to perform will be the handling of these subcontracts and the possible implementing and testing of new standard software releases which these agreements generally cover. It should be noted that it is not automatic that these should be taken and in any case it is a customer's decision (see Chapter A13).

Fault fixing maintenance for 'special-to-project' software, if the supplier is responsible for it, is initially (during the first few months of the warranty period) best provided by retaining on site maintenance programming and testing personnel, who were members of the original project team. Special-to-project software should reveal most of its major discrepancies in these first few months of operation. After this time the incidence of discrepancies does not justify a site presence, or even having staff assigned full time to the project. This presents problems because even if the customer is prepared to pay for staff to be on full-time stand-by (ignoring any suggestion of working unsocial hours) the staff themselves, if they are of the right calibre, will become dissatisfied and move on. The only real solution is for the supplier to have a general special-to-project software maintenance department with its members acquiring a working knowledge of the software by being assigned to project teams during the later stages of projects.

Assuming that the supplier is taking total responsibility for system maintenance, but subcontracting the maintenance of standard hardware and software, his personnel should have the skills described in the Personnel Requirements section at the end of this chapter.

All agreements between customer and supplier should specify the suppliers' and subcontractor's requirements for office and workshop space; spares stores; power and environmental conditions; computer time; and tools (hardware and software) on the customer's premises.

PERSONNEL REQUIREMENTS

Warranty and maintenance will be carried out by the personnel given below with the qualities listed.

COMPUTER

(Maintenance programmers and testers):

1. General computer knowledge.
2. Some applications knowledge.
3. Significant system knowledge.

ENGINEERING

1. General engineering knowledge.
(2) Significant system knowledge.
(3) Ability to set in motion appropriate manufacturer's support.

SECTION C
MANAGEMENT PROCEDURES

CHAPTER C1

CONFIGURATION MANAGEMENT AND CHANGE CONTROL

A computer system consists of a number of elements (pieces of equipment, modules of software, people, etc.). A significant number of interfaces must exist between these elements if they are collectively to provide the desired function. Loss of a single interface can, in turn, mean a loss, in part or in total, of this required functionality. Therefore, to ensure this functionality is provided, the relevant manager must have knowledge of which elements interface with which and the effect they have on each other. Configuration management provides this knowledge and hence the means of controlling a system's (generally a computer system's) environment.

All personnel connected with the system will be concerned with configuration management but the administration of configuration management will require a special configuration management function. This will be manned by administration/clerical personnel with good organizational knowledge and some technical knowledge. Management will take decisions on the data collected and collated by this function. During a system implementation the system build team will usually perform the configuration management function.

The operation of configuration management requires that the boundaries of the system should be clearly defined. Generally anything that can impact the operation, within these boundaries, will be under configuration management. However, it is sensible not to interpret this definition too strictly so that items like office furniture and general stationery are not included. Elements that must be included are

1. Operational items:
Staffing—number/grades/quality; procedures; requirements and changes implemented/being implemented/planned; documents; equipment (communications, computers, etc.) software; equipment/software documentation; interface control specifications; change procedures; staff training; staff management.
2. Support items:*
Staffing—number/grades/quality; procedures; documents; equipment (communications, computers, etc.); software; staff training; staff management; finances; work services—building, power supplies, environment.

*In this context include maintenance and development.

Configuration management works by having all elements of the system documented in a section of the system description at functional specification level; (if the contractual functional specification does not cover all the system elements the customer should have it extended until it does). An index is held which shows the connection between sections describing elements which have a connection one with another. Thus if one element of the system is changed the index will show all other elements that might require action taken on them if the correct interfaces, hence functionality, of the system are to be preserved. The actual sections will tell if indeed action requires taking and if so its nature.

Under configuration management, change control will act so that anyone wishing to change the system will raise a formal request (see Figure C1.1) which will be passed to the configuration management function. They in turn will send copies to those responsible for the possible other elements impacted. Their responses will be collected by the configuration management function into a management case showing the change requested and the reason for it plus any reasons against, and the total costs of implementation.

If the appropriate management function agrees that the change should be implemented configuration management will co-ordinate this implementation in all affected areas of the system. Configuration management will furthermore keep a record of the current and past change states and projected future change states of the system. This will be accomplished using mark and modification numbers of equipment and their associated drawings and release numbers of software and its associated documentation. A computerized relational database is a great benefit in configuration controlling the larger systems. A spin-off benefit from change control is that if a new system functional level proves unreliable a possible remedy is for the operation to revert to the previous, presumably more reliable, functional level. All elements that were required for the previous functional level should be retained with this in mind. This refers particularly to documentation. However, the retention of any more earlier levels of documentation should be positively discouraged as they can be the source of a great deal of confusion and even system failure.

Configuration control change notes should be introduced at the system design stage of a project after the functional specifications is complete. Their contents should include:-

1. A unique reference number—given by the configuration management function.
2. Title of change.
3. Description of change—couched in functional specification language.
4. Section and version of functional specification affected.
5. Date of raising change note.
6. Proposer's name and department.
7. Proposed deadline for implementation.
8. Priority of change—operationally essential, desirable or minor.

PROJECT XYZ	CHANGE REQUEST	No.

Originator	Dept	Date

Title of change

Description of change (specification language please)

Please attach continuation pages if necessary

Specification section	Specification version	Proposed date of implementation	Priority of implementation

REVIEW COSTS	Dept	Labour	Computer time	Misc.	Total	Best rev date	
	Review Dept					Comments	
	Total	∗		∗	∗ £	∗	

IMP. COSTS	Dept	Labour	Computer time	Misc.	Total	Best imp date	
	Review Dept					Comments	
	Total	∗		∗	∗ £	∗	

IMP. INSTRUC- TIONS	To be imp.	Version	Date	Priority	Authority	Comments
	Yes †					
	No †				Budget	

∗ To be inserted by CM; originators to ignore bottom half; † delete if not applicable

Figure C1   Sample Change Request Form

9. Reviewers of the change note will add reviewer's name and department.
10. Impact of change on reviewer's element of system   section of functional specification to be referenced.
11. Recommended date of implementation with constraints.
12. Cost and timescale for implementary charge for the reviewer's element.

132

There will be an option for an affected department on a first pass to put the costs of reviewing the change and not to actually review it. In this context it must be remembered that even the potential existence of a change diverts thinking and hence distracts from effective effort on a project.

CHAPTER C2

DISCREPANCY REPORTING

The manager of a computer project needs an objective means of assessing the reliability of the elements in the system. In particular he/she needs to know how close he/she is to reaching the stage where the system will pass its acceptance tests. Discrepancy reporting provides an objective method of doing both. The word 'discrepancy' is deliberately chosen because the 'fault' or 'bug' it represents is a discrepancy between how the system performs and how it should perform as documented in the appropriate functional specification. The benefits of discrepancy reporting are:

1. A method of showing the reliability and the trend in reliability of a system, in an objective way avoiding confusing subjective opinions.
2. Information for the manager in deciding where he should deploy resources for discrepancy correcting.
3. A convenient way of referring to discrepancies (simply quote reference number) and a ready means of avoiding wasted resources through over-reporting of the same discrepancy.
4. Assistance in the early detection and resolution of discrepancies when it is easier to do so, and thus saving significant time and resources during the later stages of the project.
5. Historical data for more accurate future estimating and planning.

Discrepancy reporting is the responsibility of everyone connected with a system; however, in implementation it will primarily be done by the test team. The co-ordination and circulation of discrepancy reports and the production of summary documents will be the responsibility of the discrepancy reporting function. This will be staffed by personnel possessing administrative/clerical skills. They will have significant knowledge of the organization with some technical knowledge. During an implementation the discrepancy reporting function will most probably be handled by the system build team.

With most computer projects, discrepancy reporting will be mainly concerned with special-to-project elements. These will normally be software elements with the discrepancies in them referred to in the vernacular as bugs.

However, discrepancy reporting will still be required for standard and off-the-shelf items and, although the methods of fixing problems with items in this category may be different, they should still be catalogued in the same way as special-to-project items. Indeed all items that go to make up the system should be subject to discrepancy reporting, including staff, procedures, documentation, test plans, etc. In the case of staff, care should be taken to see that the discrepancy reporting system does not become a visible public measure of an individual's performance. No third-party names should appear on a discrepancy report. If it is decided to use discrepancy reporting as a means of providing management data, these data should be held confidentially. Generally, however, it is recommended that data should not be used in that way because it will inhibit individuals from raising discrepancy reports.

It is important to note in this context that anyone at any time can raise a discrepancy report against any aspect of the system. Discrepancy reporting is not only confined to testing.

All discrepancies will be documented on a standard form, an example of which is shown in Figure C2, which will require submission of the following information.

1. A unique reference number—given by the discrepancy reporting function.
2. Priority—system operationally unworkable; system serious malfunction, etc.
3. Title of discrepancy
4. Description of discrepancy—full explanation with evidence (system log, discrepancy etc.) if available.
5. Element—the element and sub-element at fault should be identified if *positively known*.
6. Version and status—the version or modification number, etc. of the element of the system thought responsible or the overall system version number should be given as should the status of the system (operational, test or training).
7. Originator—the name and department of the person who observed the discrepancy.
8. Date and time—The date and time at which the discrepancy occurred should be recorded.

The discrepancy report form should be completed by the person observing the discrepancy. It should then be sent to the discrepancy report function. They will add a unique reference number and send copies to the team or teams responsible for the element producing the discrepancy, who after consulting with the author of the discrepancy report will effect a solution. Among the possible solutions are:

1. The problem is fixed and after testing it is agreed that it is fixed. At which point the file on it should be closed.

135

PROJECT XYZ		DISCREPANCY REPORT		No.	*
Originator			Dept	Date	
Specification section affected		System version	System status	Priority	
Title of discrepancy				Elements of system	
Description					
Support data attached	Y	N	Relevant tapes and discs saved	Numbers	

ZZZZZZZZZZZZZZZZZZZZZZZZZZZZZZZZZZZZZZZZZZZZZZZZZZZZZZZZZZZZZZZZZZZZZZZZZZZZZ

DESIGN CLOSURE	Authority	Dept	Method of closure	Comments
	Version	Date		
TEST CLOSURE	Authority	Dept	Method of closure	Comments
	Version	Date		

* To be completed by CM; originator to leave blank below ZZZZZZZZZZ

Figure C2

2. The problem may be a duplicate of an existing known one, in which case after agreement the file should be closed.
3. The fault may not be repeatable, in which case after a suitable length of time and after agreement, again the file should be closed.
4. The fault may be that the documentation is wrong and the system is performing correctly. If the document is a baseline functional description of the project a change note should be raised to bring the documentation into line and the discrepancy file closed when the change is implemented.

The discrepancy reporting function, the affected users, the implementer and the test teams should be the ones to agree on a closure. The function will retain copies of all discrepancy files with closure details included. At regular intervals they will publish and distribute to all managers a summary of outstanding discrepancies in a management document. This will list discrepancies closed since the last edition of the document and will list open discrepancies with their priorities against those responsible for elements and sub-elements.

Regular briefings will be given to interested parties by the implementation teams on their plans for solving discrepancies. This meeting will allow users to influence these plans.

Obviously the document will be used as the working tool of these briefings and it will show implementation management where and when to direct their resources.

The formalization of the above procedures will depend on the size of the project but the philosophy underlying them should be applied whatever the system.

CHAPTER C3
THE PROJECT PLAN

To manage a project successfully, data are required on all activities that lead to the successful completion of the project; the interdependencies between these activities; the responsibilities for performing these activities; the resources required to perform these activities and the dates and timescales connected with them. The amount of data is so great, that except for the very simplest projects, it is too much for one person to carry in his or her head. Even if the information is carried in several people's heads the problem of co-ordinating the information is insuperable. The only solution is to have the information co-ordinated and set out on paper in a document called a project plan.

The original project plan is, however, only a statement of intentions and there is a need to monitor how these intentions are being met. The project plan must therefore be capable of regular and expeditious amendment so that deviations from the original project plan can be quickly identified, see Figure C3.

The project plan also provides a comprehensive information source for details on the planning and progress of the project. Thus the key personnel involved with the project are spared a constant stream of enquiries.

Anyone connected with the project may be called upon to contribute to the project plan. However, the data collection, collation, and decision-taking required to produce and update a project plan from this data is the responsibility of the project management. They will be assisted in this by an administrative/clerical function, with significant organisational and some technical knowledge.

A suggested format for the project plan is to have sections which, dependent on the project, can be issued separately. The first section will chronicle the movement of changes. They will be identified by their change number and short title. They will appear as they are raised, and in the appropriate issue of the project plan the decision as to whether or not to implement them will be shown. Those changes that are to be implemented will then be shown in the plan against the version or modification state of the system in which they are to appear.

A second section will show the major contractual milestones of the project with original planned dates, revised dates, and then the dates on which they

Project XYZ	PROJECT PLAN		Plan section 5.2		Name	Support software documentation				Date 6.8.84		Page 1 of 3
Title / Doc-level	Dept	Draft comp.	To tech. pubs	To review	From review	Advance copy	To print	Available	Doc. order no. change request no.	Est. pages	Column change
Software module design documents											
1. Trio generator 4-2	SSNIS	20.7.84	3.8.84C	10.8.84C	24.8.84	31.8.84	7.9.84	21.9.84	CR107,108 116	80	C, D, F, I
2. Compool analyser 4-2	SSNIS	27.7.84C	10.8.84	17.8.84	31.8.84	7.9.84	14.9.84	28.9.84	CR107,108 116,123	80	H, I
3. Library analyser 4-2	SSNIS	27.7.84C	10.8.84	17.8.84	31.8.84	7.9.84	14.9.84		CR107,108 123	50	H
4. Background utilites	SSNIS	3.9.84C	17.8.84	24.8.84	7.9.84	14.9.84	21.9.84		CR107,108	50	G, H
A	B	C	D	E	F	G	H	I	J	K	L

Figure C3 Sample Project Plan Page—With Entries.

were actually achieved. These major milestones will be reflected in the third section of the plan, which will have chapters dealing with each aspect of the system.

There will be a section on design, showing dates by which key decisions have to be taken, dates for the completion of design reviews, etc. There will normally be three sections on software—operational, support and diagnostic. There will be a section on engineering, which in larger projects will be broken down into further sections such as computer hardware and communications equipment. Testing, training, etc. will also have one or more sections.Generally the section structure will conform to the organizational structure of the project team with a section for each line manager's responsibilities. These responsibilities will be indicated in the plan and they will show not only supplier responsibilities but also customer responsibilities (usually shown separately).

Each section will show activities required for the project with the dates for each aspect of the activity.For example:

	Design	Code	Test
MODULE XYZ ORIGINAL VERSION	10/10/84	11/11/84	5/1/85

The software sections will normally show module testing as being part of their activity. Also the work on each software module will be shown under the general heading for a particular version. With each module, for a version, will go the dates for the incorporation of particular changes.

The schedule for builds and system tests will be shown in a separate section. Standing instructions will tell those responsible for modules the cut-off dates and times for particular builds.

The plan will cover the work of peripheral support activities such as typing, technical publication, buying, maintenance, etc.

All dates will be against stages where progress can be identified, e.g 'MODULE XYZ coding complete'. Normally, start times will not be highlighted and percentage completion estimations totally avoided. As a general principle the first version of the project plan should be drawn up, after contract signature, by the project manager assisted by those who produced the system design and implementation plan for the tender and those members of his project team already in post. At this early stage it will, of necessity, be mostly incomplete at the detail level, but as the project proceeds, these details will be completed.

It is recommended that critical path or PERT techniques are used in the planning stage. Some degree of automation using a computer program is possible here, but it should be noted that in general manufacturer's packages are too complex for this purpose.

Timescale and resource estimates are best done by those who will be responsible for doing the work to achieve them using the techniques sug-

140

gested in Chapter B4. All team managers will be responsible for completing their own sections. These will be submitted for project management approval and top-level planning to the administrative/clerical function responsible for collating returns, producing them and then circulating them.

The updated project plan, with completion suitably indicated as well as new entries, will be circulated *weekly* to all departmental managers associated with the project, including services such as typing pools, technical publications, etc.

The plan will be used among other things as the working document for the progress meetings as described in Chapter A10.

Although the above project plan is aimed at the larger projects, say in excess of 20 man years of effort, it is useful discipline to produce one even for the smaller projects. These will be condensed and the procedures less formalized. However, the discipline should still be gone through.

CHAPTER C4

FINANCIAL MANAGEMENT

At various points in this book, management procedures and the organizations to carry out these management procedures have been referred to. These management procedures are: configuration management; change control; discrepancy control; project planning. The organizations to carry these out in the customer's organization are: the steering committee; the project teams for different stages. The organizations administering procedure like configuration management, change control, discrepancy control and project planning will be generally part of a total project administration function which will be closely allied to the system build team.

However, there is one administrative procedure that this group does not perform, that is providing financial data on the project, albeit the resources referenced in the project plan will be directly converted into costs expressed in monetary terms.

During the implementation of a turnkey, the supplier's costs will be charged in monetary terms according to the agreed payments plan with variations as agreed. Therefore the intermittent extra presence of the financial function in the customer's monitoring team, as suggested in Chapter A10, will be sufficient to administer the financial management of the supplier's element of the project during this stage. However, even during this stage and during the other stages of the project, the expenditure of the customer's resources hence money will not be inconsiderable.

Therefore throughout the life of the project there will be a requirement to administer and manage the financial (sometimes referred to as business) affairs of the project.

It is possible that the administration will be performed using the general budgetary control organization and methods of the customer's organization. However, because computer projects cut across departmental, product, etc. boundaries, it may be necessary to set up a financial administration dedicated to the project, within the customer's project teams themselves. The function of this administration, however it is performed, will be to advise the customer's project manager of actual and projected expenditure against planned expenditure. It is then the project manager's remit to take decisions to see that the project's financial objectives are met.

The financial plan and objectives will have been agreed and set by the steering committee as a result of the feasibility report. They will generally be revised at the end of the functional definition, design and acceptance stages. All figures in the plan will carry an element for contingency and a formula for variation due to inflation.

There are several project management methodologies that lean towards the provision of financial or business data. However, if an organization's existing procedures can adequately keep financial control of a project the addition of one of these methodologies may only add to the administrative costs of the project.

Finally, whatever the administrative or management procedures, it is important that they do not become an end in themselves and distract from the real objectives of the project.

SECTION D
CHECKLISTS

CHAPTER D1

OPERATIONAL REQUIREMENT REQUEST

The items to be considered when requesting an Operational Requirement Study are the same as those that are to be included in the document that reports such a study. These items are as follows:

1. Project title and short description.
2. User identification.
3. Study teams' terms of reference:
    (a) aims, objectives, purpose, and scope of study.
    (b) Constraints, costs, interfaces, hardware, software, and timescales.
    (c) Method of reporting, Who? Where?
    (d) Resources to be used for study.
    (e) Planning and progress control method for study.
4. Resource requirements
    (a) Manpower management, staff and consultants, administrative.
    (b) Logistics—accommodation, computer time, etc.
    (c) Finance—detailed budget for study.
5. Timetable—including reporting points.
6. Departmental involvements in study.

CHAPTER D2
FEASIBILITY STUDY

The items to be considered when undertaking a feasibility study are the same as are to be included in the document that reports on the study, namely the feasibility report. These items are:

1. Project title and short description.
2. Conclusion.
3. Justification. | Technical, financial, social
4. Feasibility. |
5. Future activities:
   (a) Assuming the project is justified and feasible—the way ahead, funding, staffing, timescales, etc.
   (b) Assuming the project is not justified or feasible—alternatives if possible.

CHAPTER D3

OPERATIONAL REQUIREMENT

The items to be considered when producing an operational requirement are those topics that should be included in the resultant document. These items are:

1. Project title and short description.
2. Background
   (a) History of requirement.
   (b) Terms of reference of operational requirement.
   (c) State of the applications art.
   (d) Other systems/prototypes, etc.
3. Functions required—with desirability.
4. Data and process—structures, flow and interrelationship (in diagrammatic form).
5. Performance requirements:
   (a) Maximum loadings.
   (b) Response times.
   (c) Deadlines.
6. Availability/reliability requirements:
   (a) Percentage availability.
   (b) Maximum recovery time.
7. Expandability potential requirements:
   (a) Physical.
   (b) Functional.
8. Security Requirements:
   (a) Loss of data.
   (b) Illegal access.
9. Staffing and organizational details:
   (a) Quantity.
   (b) Quality.
   (c) Responsibilities.
   (d) Training requirements.
10. Timescale, phasing and system introduction requirements.

11. Documentation requirements.
12. Standards and References.

It is optional, but the feasibility and business case including financial/commercial justification could also be added.

CHAPTER D4

INVITATIONS TO TENDER

The items to be considered when producing an invitation to tender are the same as those that should be included in the document itself. They are:

1. Project title and short description.
2. Tendering procedures:
   (a) Closing date.
   (b) Where to be sent.
   (c) Method of packaging.
   (d) Number of copies required.
   (e) Format of tenders (including prices)—see Checklist D7.
   (f) Contact points and names.
   (g) Arrangements for meetings/presentations, etc.
   (h) Financial guarantee requirements (if any).
3. Operational requirement:
   (a) As in checklist D3, although such items as financial/commercial justification might be removed if considered confidential and/or irrelevant.
   (b) The supplier should be asked to comment on the Operational Requirement, particularly its adequacy for *fully* specifying his task.
   (c) The supplier should be asked to show how his design will meet the operational requirement.
4. Technical requirement:
   (a) Details of customer's general computer policy (e.g. preferred languages, manufacturers).
   (b) Site details—volume, area, floor loading, power supplies, environment, access, potential hazards, etc. with plans.
   (c) Specifications for interfaces with other systems.
   (d) Details of existing facilities which might be used for the project and/or its later support.
   (e) Details of data files or databases to be set up.
   (f) Details of any constraints on the supplier's offering.
   (g) Suggested criteria for acceptance.
   (h) Customer staff availability during project and after for support and operation—numbers and quality.

(i) Requests for technical information in the tender—see Checklists D4, D5 and D6.

(j) Requests for a benchmark test to be performed with its specification.

5. Implementation requirement:

(a) Customer's timescale requirements.

(b) Customers' preferences in the implementation strategy (e.g. where it is carried out; team structure, methodologies, etc).

(c) Requests for implementation information in the tender—see Checklists D5 and D6.

6. Support requirements:

(a) Warranty and maintenance requirements.

(b) Requests for information on hardware, software, staff and procedures to support staff.

7. Contract requirement—A draft contract – see Section E.

CHAPTER D5

TENDER

Commercially sensitive data will have to be considered while a tender is being prepared, particularly internal costings. Also information about competitors and possible subcontractors. Otherwise the items to be considered are those topics that will be included in the tender itself. They are:

1. Project title and short description.
2. Prices:
   (a) Material—list of deliverables with individual price.
   (b) Labour—including software development.
   (c) Commercial—price variation, cost of money, licences, insurance, etc.
3. Company details:
   (a) Turnover—number of employees, ownership.
   (b) Previous relevant experience.
   (c) Subcontractors with details.
4. Operational requirements:
   (a) Comments.
   (b) Adequacy for implementation.
5. Technical offering:
   (a) Glossary of terms.
   (b) Operational understanding
   (c) System design—hardware and software configuration and software and data structures.
   (d) Hardware—both computer and communication for operational support and training.
   (e) Software—operational, support (standard or special-to-project, etc.), training and diagnostic, language, structure standard, etc.
   (f) Documentation—hardware, software and procedures for user and support staff usage.
   (g) Performance calculations (load and response times) including recovery and fallback. Results of benchmark test.
   (h) Reliability calculations, including recovery and fallback.
   (i) Special features—e.g. security if not covered in system design.
   (j) Staffing requirements, operational and support.

    (k) Training to be offered—*modus operandi.*
    (l) Warranty and maintenance to be offered—*modus operandi.*
    (m) Installation and access requirements.
    (n) Quality assurance.

6. Implementation programme
    (a) Staffing—project manager and key team members' curriculum vitae.
    (b) Activities—bar or PERT chart showing all activities and responsibilities including those of customer.
    (c) Provision of support facilities both hardware and software including data preparation.
    (d) Setting up of data files and databases.
    (e) Testing and acceptance testing.
    (f) Introduction requirements.
    (g) Management procedures.
    (h) Access requirements—before and after handover.
    (i) Milestones with dates.

7. Technical compliance statement.
8. Contractual compliance statement.
9. Standards and references.

CHAPTER D6

TENDER EVALUATION

Those evaluating tenders should address the following questions. They are basically in the same order as the tender checklist D5. No attempt has been made to give the questions weightings or suggest whether the requirements are mandatory, desirable or simply nice to have.

PRICE

Does the price cover the elements of the requirement?
    Are all hardware and software items required included in the price?
    Are all commercial aspects taken cognizance of in the price, including variations, cost of money, contingency against risks, cost of insurance, cost of licences, etc.?

COMPANY DETAILS

Is this company sufficiently stable both commercially and financially to complete the project and provide support for the requisite period afterwards?
    Is this company sufficiently committed to the project to the same ends?
    Do the company and its employees have sufficient expertise to the same ends?
    Does the company have a sufficiency of this expertise uncommitted which it will commit to the project to the same ends?
    Are the same questions true for all subcontractors
    Does the prime contractor have a satisfactory working relationship with all subcontractors? (Previous examples of a harmonious working relationship would be useful.)

OPERATIONAL REQUIREMENT

Does this company show a sufficient understanding of the operational requirement to enable it successfully to complete the project on time? (This question can be broken down into questions about specific areas or functions.)

Do the company's comments on the adequacy of the operational requirement reveal the necessary understanding of what resources will be involved in producing the required system on time?

TECHNICAL OFFERING

Does the tenderer show an adequate understanding of the operational aspects of the system?

Do the operational software and associated data structure design show an adequacy, particularly in volume, to perform all functions required?

Does the hardware proposed have sufficient capacity to handle the operational software and data and meet the performance requirements?

Is there sufficient spare capacity to accommodate errors in the estimation of the amount of operational software and data required?

Does the design meet the required extension potential requirements?

Do the hardware and software proposed have the capability of meeting the fallback and recovery criteria specified with sufficient margin for error?

Do the benchmark results support the supplier's claims?

Do the hardware and software proposed meet the reliability criteria specified with sufficient margin for error?

Do the hardware, software and procedures proposed meet the security criteria of the system, including separation of operational data from test and training data?

How adequate is the system when the same questions are asked for support, training and maintenance requirements?

How adequate is the design for the realistic worst case when the same questions are asked for the possible case of operation, support, training and maintenance running combined?

Is the documentation proposed adequate to cover the operation, support and training function of the system; and is it to the standard specified?

Are the staff and procedures proposed adequate, both in numbers and quality, to use the system so as to provide the operational service required and to go on providing it?

Is the warranty proposed sufficient to give confidence that it will meet all possible problems during the warranty period?

Is the length of the warranty programme sufficient to expose and corect a very high proportion of teething troubles the system will experience?

Is the maintenance offered sufficient to give minimal risk that the system will not perform continuously to the specified standard?

Are the works services planned adequate for the installation (including access) of the equipment with contingency capacity?

IMPLEMENTATION PROGRAMME

Are sufficient staff allocated to the project to see its successful and timely completion? (Including no unreasonable delay in setting up the supplier's team.)

Are the staff to be allocated to the project of sufficient intellect, experience and motivation?

Are the proposed project milestones realistic and do they meet the time-scale requirements?

Are project activities identified to a sufficient degree that one can be confident that no significant items are forgotten or ignored?

Are the responsibilities allocated for different activities reasonable; and are the ones allocated to the customer amenable and capable of being performed by him in the suggested timescale?

Are the support facilities—hardware, software, people and procedures including data preparation—adequate for production (particularly programming) and testing at *all* stages of the project?

Are the arrangements for setting up data files and databases adequate both to support and meeting timescales for testing and full operation of the system?

Are the tests and acceptance test proposed for the system along with their supporting staff, facilities, tools and procedures sufficient to give confidence in the system totally meeting its requirements?

Will the proposed plans for the introduction of the system work and cause minimum disruption?

Are there management procedures for the project and the staff, and logistics to carry them out satisfactorily?

Does the technical compliance statement support all the above answers?

Does the contractual compliance statement give any cause for concern that the supplier will not endeavour to meet his obligations?

Does the contractual compliance statement indicate that the supplier is unwilling to shoulder his share of technical and financial risk on the project?

REPORTING

Once the priorities and weightings have been applied, a report should be produced showing each supplier's score against the above questions. The methods of calculating the final order should then be shown and the conclusion with any factors, not already covered, given.

CHAPTER D7
FUNCTIONAL SPECIFICATION

The items to be considered when producing a functional specification are the same as those that should be included in the document itself. They are:
1. Project title and short description.
2. Glossary of terms.
3. Description of the application (as for the operational requirement).
4. Overall description of the design including all major elements both hardware and software including the chosen language.
5. Detailed description of the design, including:
   (a) User stations—types, permitted use, access, numbers.
   (b) Interfaces—control consoles, other computer systems, networks.
   (c) Transactions—message formats, data conventions, responses, permitted/forbidden transactions, automatic transactions.
   (d) Outputs—form, route, time.
   (e) Database—form, preparation and alteration, access.
6. System parameters.
7. Priorities.
8. Undesired events—warnings, precautions, response.
9. Performance—figures for capacity, accuracy, response times.
10. Availability/reliability—criteria, times to fix.
11. Support facilities—bureau, testing, training—function, method, input, output for each.

CHAPTER D8

SYSTEM DESIGN SPECIFICATION

The items to be considered when producing a system design specifiction are the same as those that should be included in the document itself. They are:

1. Project title and short description
2. Glossary of terms
3. Summary of the project and implementation:
   (a) Functions and performance requirements, its benefits (not quantified for commercial in confidence reasons).
   (b) Details of the implementation: manpower, costs, schedule.
4. Overview showing how the various hardware and software elements fit together and with the user functions.
5. Description of the hardware both computer and communications down to unit level.
6 Description of the software—operational, support and diagnostic. This will be divided up into standard and special-to-project. The interrelationships will be shown along with the modular structure. The data structure will be shown and all conventions used carefully explained. Common variables will be listed with their type.
7. Procedures associated with the support of the system will be identified. These will include start-up recovery and fallback security, support, testing and training mode set-up and use, etc.
8. Staff required for the support of the system will be identified, their number, structures and knowledge requirements will also be shown.

This document is written as the top-level technical response to the functional requirement. It should therefore mention, and be cross-referenced to, all items mentioned in the requirement. It also forms the peak of the system documentation, and in this case it should serve as an overview and bring all aspects of the design together.

CHAPTER D9
TEST AND ACCEPTANCE

To conduct testing (including acceptance testing) in general or to perform a particular test the following are required:

1. A configuration sufficiently representative of the operational configuration.
2. Sufficient time available for testing on the configuration.
3. A project or general bureau available for supporting tasks.
4. Adequate and timely service on bureau.
5. Documented support software for testing and analysing results as Chapter B15.
6. Experienced computer operators and support staff (including data preparation) to run test and bureau support tasks.
7. Sufficient computer consumables.
8. General and specific test plans.
9. Quality control procedures.
10. Test scripts and anticipated results (or in the general case, experienced personnel to support them), data files or databases (if applicable).
11. Experienced personnel to compare actual and anticipated results.

The items that have to be considered for testing (including acceptance testing) are the same as those that will be included in the test plan. They are:

1. Test philosophy—general pass criteria.
2. Test list—including elements of system tested in each test.
3. Test programme—sequence, level interdependencies and dates (identical to development plan test section).
4. Test tools
   (a) Hardware.
   (b) Software.
5. Data files or databases with comprehesiveness criteria met.
6. Test personnel
   (a) Test team—structure/responsiblities.
   (b) Sign off, responsibilities.

7. Test procedures:
   (a) Test and result scripting.
   (b) Test set-up.
   (c) Test sign-off/rejection.
   (d) Arbitration (particularly for non-system tests).
8. Acceptance testing:
   (a) Will follow and mostly refer to the above except there will be obvious differences in areas such as sign-off.
   (b) Responsibilities.

Each test will have a test specification containing:

1. Item to be tested (e.g. module, function, system, document).
2. Purpose of test—pass criteria, relevance.
3. Dependencies of test (stand alone, test prerequisites, etc).
4. Conditions for test.
5. Time and date of test.
6. Test script including standard items and file.
7. Anticipated results (console and other peripheral outputs).
8. Test configuration and tools required with version/mod level.
9. Analysis requirements.
10. Requirements for repetition (A) upon failure, (B) upon success.

After every test a test report will be produced. A test report will contain the following information:

1. Project.
2. Test title.
3. Items tested.
4. Modification or version number.
5. Date and department/person carrying out the test.
6. Result of Test.
7. Observations (this will normally be a list of discrepancy reports).
8. Test scripts, test results expected; tools used; all with modification or version numbers.

CHAPTER D10

INSTALLATION

The items that will have to be considered during installation are listed here. Only those items requiring attention will be referenced with dates, etc., in the appropriate section of the project plan. Items to be considered are:

1. Floor space.
2. Floor bearing strength.
3. Floor construction (for cabling).
4. Floor coverings.
5. Floor oscillation.
6. Ceiling height.
7. Air conditioning.
8. Ventilation and dust filtering.
9. Lighting.
10. Fire protection.
11. Fire-alarms, fire-fighting apparatus.
12. Noise limits.
13. Room cleaning.
14. Electricity:
    (a) Power input.
    (b) Mains connection conditions (frequency, voltages with tolerances).
    (c) Current distribution.
    (d) Relays.
    (e) Safety precautions.
    (f) Power failure precautions.
15. Access:
    (a) Maximum size restriction on access route.
    (b) Maximum weight restriction on access route.
    (c) Capabilities of human or mechanical aids.

Some projects may have to conform to installation standards for a particular country, organization or building. These will be building regulations, electrical regulations, etc. These should be consulted and the appropriate actions needed to conform should be inserted in the project plan. Some very large projects may have their own installation standards. These may be specified in a separate document (under configuration control).

160

CHAPTER D11

TRAINING

A checklist follows for the computer-related training requirements. This checklist will serve also for the computer-related requirements of a particular lesson or session. The diversity of support personnel training is such that it is not possible to give one here. However, one should be drawn up for each project and become part of that discipline's training manual.

1. Configuration sufficiently representative of operational system.
2. Sufficient time available for training on this configuration.
3. Configuration loaded with software identical to operational system and representative data.
4. Impossible for trainee to corrupt operational software and/or data.
5. On-line VDU or other appropriate device dedicated to student.
6. Sufficient computer consumables available.
7. Instructor is experienced and trained.
8. Configuration is manned by experienced operators.
9. Course and individual lesson(s)* have been planned.
10. Training manual* available.
    * All these items are co-ordinated.

Where a significant amount of training is required a training specification should be produced. It will contain:

1. Details of all courses and their applicability.
2. Details of all course requirements, particularly documentation.
3. Details of all course prerequisites for students.

The schedule of course dates will be shown in the training section of the project plan.

QUALITY ASSURANCE

Comprehensive procedures should be laid down to ensure that quality exists throughout the system. It is the function of quality assurance to see that these procedures exist and are acted upon. This will include all the procedures referenced in this book. Procedures that are of particular importance are:

1. Comprehensive specification of the application and how it is to be accommodated in the system being implemented.
2. Comprehensive specification of the system design to implement the specified application.
3. Comprehensive specification of the standards to be used in that system design process.
4. Comprehensive standard methods for the selection/production of hardware and standard software to meet the design.
5. Comprehensive standard methods for the production of special-to-project software to meet the design.
6. Comprehensive standard methods for the installation of hardware and software.
7. Comprehensive standards for the selection and training of staff to produce, use and support the system.
8. Comprehensive standard methods for the collection, integration and input of data, particularly long-term data, to the system for testing, acceptance testing, and operation of the system.
9. Comprehensive standardized documentation for all the above aspects of the system.
10. Comprehensive documentation standards.
11. Comprehensive management of the production of the system, including: project standards; project plan; configuration management and change control; discrepancy reporting.
12. Comprehensive testing of the system in part and in total.

CHAPTER D13

GOING OPERATIONAL

Before going operational *all* the following conditions must apply:

1. All relevant management agreed and committed to going operational on given dates.
2. Functional level of system to go operational is that which actual operational day-to-day users have agreed to.
3. Acceptance testing complete to specified criteria.
4. Sufficient staff, both operational and support, with reserves, trained and available.
5. All systems data available and identical, where appropriate with data of previous system (manual or automated).
6. Support arrangement available, proven and tested, so as to be capable of sustaining operational system.
7. Adequate financial resources including insurance available to sustain system until next appropriation cycle.
8. Adequate stocks of consumables available commensurate with order cycle.
9. Cut-over plan from old system, if required, ready for enactment.
10. All affected parties briefed, sufficiently well in advance, as to time and date system goes operational.
11. Should the system not perform satisfactorily, a tried and tested method of working (probably the former) exists, and the method of changing to it is proven and available.

CHAPTER D13

GOING OPERA

CHAPTER D14

POST PROJECT REVIEW

The items to be considered when undertaking a post project review are the same as those that are to be included in the document that reports on such a review. They are:

1. The project title and description.
2. Assessment whether the original system objectives were correct and how far they have been met in practice.
3. Highlight areas capable of improvement.
4. Endorse good practices.
5. Identify and assess any operational problems encountered.
6. State whether the claimed benefits have been achieved.

CHAPTER D15

SUPPORT AND DEVELOPMENT FACILITY

The support and development facility will have the following elements:

1. Hardware—as dictated by the bureau, testing, training and documentation needs of the particular system.
2. Software—as itemized in Chapter B15 plus a version of the operational software for training.
3. Staff—as indicated in the Personnel Requirements section of B15. (NB. Where the operation and support roles can be accommodated on the same configuration, economies in operational staff could be made – although care must be taken with different attitudes and priorities.)
4. Procedures—these will include:
    (a) Operation of the computer.
    (b) Maintenance procedures, both planned and emergency.
    (c) Data control procedures (including media librarianship and data preparation).
    (d) Job submission procedures.
    (e) Scheduling procedures.
    (f) Procedures for user/facility communication and liaison.
    (g) Consumables provision.
5. Documentation—the facility should have up-to-date copies of all documentation associated with the project/system. The facility itself will have a procedures manual containing specifications of the procedures referred to above.

The general procedures connected with the system will be documented in user manuals, operations manuals, data manuals, training manuals etc. They will generally be culled from the functional specification and design specification. Their variety and content will be dependent on the particular project. They will at all times be under configuration management.

CHAPTER D16
PROJECT STANDARDS

The project methods and standards will be detailed in this document. It will contain:

1. Project title and short description.
2. The project teams, both customer's and supplier's organization reporting structures and responsibilities.
3. The project methodologies particularly for requirements specification, software design and programming.
4. Programming standards—routine sizes, naming conventions, etc.
5. Documentation standards.
6. Data collection standards.
7. Source software control procedures.
8. Use of standard packages.
9. Project management requirements—e.g. project plan entries, discrepancy reports, changes reports, progress meetings, etc.
10. *Ad hoc* documentation—the procedures for dealing with *ad hoc* documentation, minutes, letters, memos, etc. should be included.

HARDWARE (COMMUNICATIONS AND COMPUTERS) DOCUMENTATION

A specification for each type of unit of hardware, computer or communications, will be available within the documentation of the system. As most items of hardware are standard the manufacturer's normal technical literature will suffice. However, all hardware specifications will contain the following:

1. Title/description of unit.
2. Function and performance.
3. Physical size, environmental and power supply requirements.
4. Operating instructions.
5. Maintenance requirements.
6. Interfaces with other hardware/software elements of system.

SOFTWARE (INCLUDING DATA STRUCTURE) DOCUMENTATION

A specification for each software module will be included in the documentation of the system:

1. Title/description of module.
2. Function.
3. Size in storage.
4. Variables used and their type.
5. Data input and output by module.
6. Interface with hardware.
7. Common files/arrays, etc., accessed. These are described in the systems specification.
8. Files/arrays, etc. specific to module with description and size.
9. Error messages generated.
10. Other modules, subroutines or functions called.
11. Listing—with comprehensive comment statements.
12. Test data for stand-alone module with anticipated results.
13. Performance—path-lengths for all main functions.
14. Data elements (e.g. database) will be documented in a similar way with sizing and dependency information paramount. Default options will be shown.

CHAPTER D19

WARRANTY AND MAINTENANCE

The main points to be considered for the provision of warranty and maintenance are:

1. Responsibilities for maintenance of different elements.
2. Users should have a single point of contact.
3. An arbitrator is required where fault responsibility is disputed.
4. The warranty/maintenance cover requirements.
5. The response times to calls for maintenance.
6. Spares holding requirements.
7. Requirements for workshop adjacent to computer(s).
8. Scheduling of planned maintenance.
9. Access by supplier's personnel.

The procedures for the call-out of maintenance personnel should be specified as part of the functional specification. For convenience they may be extracted and form part of smaller user's manuals, etc. Care should be taken to see that they are up to date using configuration management.

CHAPTER D20

DOCUMENTS

The principal documents to describe all aspects of the system and where they are described are as follows:

Document	Chapters containing major references
Design specification	B7, D8
Feasibility report	A4, D2
Functional specification	A9, B6, D7
Hardware documentation	B14, D17
Installation manual	B9, D10
Invitation to tender	A6, D4
Operational requirement request	D1
Operational requirement	A5, D3
Procedures handbook	B14, B15
Project plan	C3
Project standards	D16
Quality assurance plan	B13, D12
Software documentation	B14, D18
Test plan	B10, B12, D9
Training manual	B14
User's handbook	B14
Post-project review	D14

SECTION E

CONTRACT CLAUSES

Although the previous sections have detailed what will be agreed between customer and supplier and these are simply confirmed by clauses referencing appropriate sections of the invitation to tender and the response thereto, there are purely contractual matters requiring agreement. This section contains the major ones and describes the customer's and supplier's attitudes to them. An indication of what an agreeable position might be is also included but abnormal circumstances could of course alter this. Although this section is principally of use in the procurement situation, it gives a useful guide to the inter-departmental wrangling which can occur if a project is executed within the organization. Means should be found of avoiding them and hence expediting the project. English contract law is used and terminology is used. However, the general principles will apply to other legal systems.

Clause	Customer attitude	Supplier attitude	Suggested consensus
Information	The supplier must have this information if he is to do his job, but a confidentiality clause must be present to secure purchaser rights	The supplier must have this information	The customer will freely supply the information the supplier requires to do his job subject to a confidentiality clause
Accommodation	The supplier must have accommodation to perform his work on site. Caveats may be required so that the purchaser is not inconvenienced in any way	Site accommodated must be provided free and be suitable for the work required to be done	Accommodation will be provided with agreed caveats detailing the description each side may place on this

(*continued*)

Clause	Customer attitude	Supplier attitude	Suggested consensus
Access	The customer will require access to the supplier's premises for inspection, etc. At the same time he may wish to restrict access to his own premises for reasons such as security. It may also be necessary for him to ask the supplier's personnel to have access during unsocial hours (e.g. for time on an operational system)	The supplier will require access to the customer's premises for site inspection, testing, installation, etc. At the same time he may wish to restrict access to his own premises for reasons of security or to prevent his staff being unnecessarily distracted from their work	The customer and supplier will agree the necessary access requirements to each others' premises. This will be couched in terms of the numbers involved, dates, times, and possibly a requirement for advance warning
Terms and conditions payment profile (please see Chapter A8)			
Imported equipment price	The customer would prefer not to have a fluctuating price	The supplier does nto want to take risks of loading the quoted price and losing sale nor does he want to lose money	The supplier will be asked to quote today's prices with agreed fixed contingency. The contract quotes this with the proviso that if the contingency proves inadequate, incremental cost is shared
Inflation	The customer would prefer not to have a fluctuating price	The supplier does not want to take risks of loading the quoted price and losing sale nor does he want to lose money	A 'fixed' price with escalation is requested where the price is linked to appropriate national index for goods and labour from a fixed

Clause	Customer attitude	Supplier attitude	Suggested consensus
			date. The schedule of deliverables should show which items of goods or labour
Delays attributable to customer	Does not want to pay out any further money	Wants compensation for cost of keeping team together longer, storage, etc.	Customer reimburses supplier for amount calculated from agreed standard charges
Delays attributable to supplier	Wants recompense for extra cost incurred through delay	Does not want further expense other than cost of keeping team together	Team kept together without extra charge and supplier reimbursed for agreed other losses up to an agreed limit of liability
Penalties	Although they act as the necessary 'stick', punitive clauses should be avoided. Incompetent suppliers will not make any provision for them while the competent will thus disadvantage themselves competitively. Not really what the customer wants		Recommended not included if above agreed
Bonuses	Customers generally against paying more money out for on-time or early delivery, etc. But in business notorious for overruns sometimes effective	Supplier welcomes them	If included should be specified carefully only against clear times and definable levels of achievement

(*continued*)

Clause	Customer attitude	Supplier attitude	Suggested consensus
Cancellation	Would wish to have clause for non-performance by supplier with costs recouped. Also would like protection from the consequences of supplier pulling out	Would wish to have protection against customer cancelling arbitrarily with resultant cost incurred and industry odiums	1. Both sides to give agreed notice period 2. Severance terms to be discussed 3. If parties do not agree, right by either party to go to named independent arbitrator
Changes	Customer wishes to have option to introduce changes but requires assurances about cost and timescale impacts	While in general welcoming changes (normally more money) they must go through an agreed procedure whereby supplier is protected against loss due to changes and liability through not meeting target deadlines	A change control mechanism as specified in Chapter C1. All quotes to be based on agreed rates. Supplier has obligation to implement all reasonable changes which have gone through change control procedure
Training (other than formal courses)	Customer wants his staff to learn from supplier's staff during implementation	Will not want to spend time training customer's staff unless allowed for in price and timescale	The number of customer's staff and their access to the supplier's staff is limited by an amount specified in the contract. Any additional training will be payed for at agreed rates
Poaching	Both parties wish to avoid loss of staff and particular problems caused by staff defecting to the other party		No poaching except by agreement for the life of the project and an agreed time afterwards

Clause	Customer attitude	Supplier attitude	Suggested consensus
Intellectual property rights	Customer might have security problems and requires protection for something he has paid for which might have revenue-earning potential	Wishes to retain the use of what is developed for further commercial advantage	Joint agreement for future commercial exploitation of product with caveat on further uses to protect each party's security interests
Force majeure	Customer does not want to pay any more for occurrences beyond his and the supplier's reasonable control	Supplier does not want to pay any more for occurrences beyond his and the customer's reasonable control	Agree clause common to both parties making them not responsible under circumstances
Liability	The customer does not wish to be held responsible for a variety of losses that the supplier could cause including death, injury, damage to property, consequential or indirect loss, etc. He does not wish to be held responsible for the supplier's financial loss, loss of profits contracts, etc. He does not want to be held responsible for the supplier infringing copyright, etc.	The supplier similarly does not wish to be held responsible for these losses caused and/or incurred by the customer, particularly as there may be a multiplication factor	A clause will be introduced into the contract whereby the customer and the supplier indemnify each other against losses of these types. A mutually agreed limit of liability should be included commensurate with the parties' insurance cover. The party giving the indemnity should have conduct and control over any claims ensuing

(continued)

176

Clause	Customer attitude	Supplier attitude	Suggested consensus
Alteration	It is in both parties' interest that only alterations to be agreement agreed by both parties are valid		A clause will be introduced restricting alterations, etc. to those jointly agreed by both parties and signed by their authorized representatives
Confidentiality	The customer does not wish the supplier to reveal any proprietary or confidential data gained about him by the supplier during the execution of the contract	Similarly the supplier will not wish this to extend to know-how and experiences gained during the execution of the contract	A clause should be included restraining each party from revealing proprietary or confidential information gained during the contract General experience, public domain or third-party knowledge should be excluded
Vesting	The customer wishes to identify items pre-delivery in the possession of the supplier as his items, particularly when he has paid for them. This is helpful if the business of the supplier is wound up or there is any attempt by the supplier to reschedule items on a production line, etc.	The supplier is against it because it restricts him in his arrangements	Except in particular circumstances it buys the purchaser little and can in fact work against him because to a certain extent it implies acceptance, possibly pre-testing. If vesting is enforced appropriate insurance should be taken out

(continued)

Clause	Customer attitude	Supplier attitude	Suggested consensus
Agreed rates	The customer would like to know the supplier's rates for such items as labour, etc. through the life of the contract (and possibly beyond if a maintenance agreement is included) so he can assess his life costs	The supplier would find it commercially impossible and dangerous so to commit himself	The supplier should be obliged to state his rates at the time of contract signature and his policy for changing them. A period of notice should be agreed for any changes in rates

GLOSSARY OF TERMS

Although an attempt has been made to keep this book free of computer industry jargon, inevitably it has proved impossible to eliminate it completely. Where possible, words and terms which might be new to the reader are explained when they first appear or a reference is given to the chapter where they are explained in the text. These generally refer to management practices, project stages or documents. However, this leaves some technical terms which are explained in this glossary.

Applications programmer   Job title for a person who writes programs that perform a particular application (generally special-to-project).

Assembler   A program which translates a low-level computer language into a form the computer can execute.

Chief programmer team   A concept for the organization of a programming team into a more clearly defined function; in particular, a chief programmer, an assistant programmer and a librarian.

Comment lines   Lines introduced into a program to describe to the human reader what the program will do at that point. They are not executed by the computer.

Compiler   A program which translates a high-level computer language into a form the computer can execute.

Computer peripheral   An element of a computer configuration peripheral to the central processor and its associated main storage. For example, a magnetic tape drive, a line printer.

Core dump analyser   A program which analyses the contents of a computer's main store and makes them to some degree intelligible to a pgorammer.

Database   A concept for a pool of data held on computer storage which may be accessed by many programs and/or many executions of a program.

Data base manager   A job title for the person charged with organizing the data held in a database

Data controller   The job title of a person responsible for preparing jobs for computer processing and controlling and co-ordinating the return of results to the relevant user.

Data processing   A term applied to the element of the computer industry which generally handles commercial systems.

178

Data processor A job title for a person who works equipment which transforms manuscript data into a computer readable form.

Debugger A program which identifies the bugs (discrepancies), usually the syntactical ones in another program.

File handler A program which manipulates files of information held on computer storage.

Fourth generation language A very high-level language more easily understood by a user than normal high-level languages.

Hardware The tangible equipment of a computer system.

Hardware monitor A piece of equipment which records and analyses the performance of a computer.

High-level language A computer language which is based towards appearing close to a conventional spoken or written language.

Job control language A computer language which enables the programmer and the operator to control the way a computer handles whole programs and groups of data.

Low-level language A computer language which is biased towards appearing close to the operating language of the computer itself.

Media librarian A job title for the person who acts as a librarian for all the removable storage media (e.g. magnetic tape) in a particular computer installation.

Operator A job title for the person who physically operates the computer.

Operating system The program that enables the hardware of a computer to perform the basic tasks that enable it to run other programs and hence do useful work.

Original equipment' manufacturer (OEM) A computer or computer parts manufacturer whose products are compatible with the products of another manufacturer who was responsibel for the design and manufacture of the original computer type.

Program design language (PDL) A system of specifying software designs. Not generally executable on a computer.

Security In a computer context, ensuring that data are not lost or are not accessed by an unauthorized user.

Software The intangible programs and data which with hardware make up a computer system.

Software module A unit of software less than a program—generally performing a homogeneous function.

Software monitor A program which records and analyses the performance of a computer system.

Source The state of a computer language as it is written.

Standard software Software that is written for use by many installations and for many projects and not special-to-project.

Structured analysis, structured design, structured programming Performance of these functions in a standard specialized way for greater efficiency of production and understanding.

180

Systems analyst   Job title for a person analysing a user's requirement.

Systems designer   Job title for a person designing a computer system.

Systems programmer   Job title for a programmer concerned with standard software—particularly the operating system, performing tasks such as tuning the system for maximum efficiency , etc.

Systems tester   Job title for a person testing a computer system.

Test harness   A program that is used to test a software module generally for functional correctness.

Test scripts (and anticipated results)   Collections of input data (with expected output data) to test that a system, or part of a system, performs as expected.

User groups   An organization of bodies using a particular computer product, formed with the objective of sharing technical information about that product and lobbying the manufacturer of that product for improvements, etc.

Visual display unit (VDU)   A computer peripheral which displays data on a television-like screen. Usually associated with a keyboard for control of data input.

VLSI circuits   Very large scale integrated circuits—the hardware technology on which computers are currently based.

BIBLIOGRAPHY

Albrecht, A. J., and Gaffney, J. E., Software function, source lines of code and development effort prediction. A software science, *IEEE Transactions on Software Engineering*, November 1983.

Arthur, L. *Measuring Programmer Productivity and Software Quality*, John Wiley.

Bentley, Colin, *Computer Project Management*, John Wiley.

Boar, B. *Application Prototyping*, John Wiley.

Boehm, Barry, *Software Engineering Economics*, Prentice-Hall.

Brooks, Fred, *The Mythical Man Month*, Addison Wesley.

Connor, Dennis, *Information Systems Specification and Design Road Map*, Prentice-Hall.

Dijkstra, E. W., *A Discipline of Programming*, Prentice-Hall.

Hetzel, William, *The Complete Guide to Software Testing*, Collins.

Jackson, M. A., *Principles of Program Design*, Academic Press.

Jones, C. B., *Software Development—a Rigorous Method*, Prentice-Hall.

Licker, Paul S., *The Art of Managing Software Development People*, John Wiley.

Marco, Tom de, *Controlling Software Projects*, Yourdon Press.

Joslin, Edward, *Computer Selection*, Addison-Wesley.

Special section on software engineering project management, *IEEE Transactions on Software Engineering*, January 1984.

Summerville, Ian, *Software Engineering*, Addison Wesley.

Weinberg, G., *The Psychology of Computer Programming*, Van Nostrand.

Yourdon, Edward, *Managing the System Life Cycle*, Yourdon Press.

Index

Phases and stages in the computer project process along with associated methods and support elements are listed in the contents. General computer job titles are described in the two chapters on *Staffing* (A3 and B2) and their appendixes and the *Glossary of Terms*.